Magic, Witchcraft, and Religion

Magic, Witchcraft, and Religion

Perspectives in the Media

THIRD EDITION

Edited by Liam D. Murphy

cognella®

SAN DIEGO

Bassim Hamadeh, CEO and Publisher

Carrie Baarns, Senior Manager, Revisions and Author Care

Kaela Martin, Project Editor

Jeanine Rees, Production Editor

Emely Villavicencio, Senior Graphic Designer

Alexa Lucido, Licensing Manager

Natalie Piccotti, Director of Marketing

Kassie Graves, Vice President of Editorial

Jamie Giganti, Director of Academic Publishing

Cover image copyright © 2020 iStockphoto LP/RomoloTavani.

Printed in the United States of America.

3970 Sorrento Valley Blvd., Ste. 500, San Diego, CA 92121

Contents

Part III.   Magical Culture   47

Part IV.   The Living Dead Among Us   67

Preface to the Third Edition

||||||||||||||||||||||||||||||||||||||||||||||||||||||||||||||||||||||||||||||||||||||||||||||||||||||||||||||||||||||||||||||||||||||||||

I n the several years that have elapsed since the second edition of *Magic, Witchcraft, and Religion in the Media* was published, many new developments in US society have ensured that religion remains at the front and center of public consciousness in this country ... and not, as we will see, for all the proverbial "right reasons." In addition to a slightly modified title, for this third edition, I've therefore decided to select my readings and base my commentary on the American religious landscape exclusively. It is true, obviously, that religious beliefs, practices, experiences, and institutions remain vital aspects of our common humanity on a global scale. Still, I felt it was necessary for this 2022 edition to draw our attention back to the ways in which religion—whether traditional or (emphatically) untraditional—indexes a spectrum of orientations toward the supernatural and transcendent while simultaneously serving as a lens to illuminate, magnify, and refract various dimensions of our fragmented and culturally divided society; these objectives are perhaps more important now than ever given our era of deep political polarization, conspiracy theory, police brutality, and pandemic.

"In the beginning" (so to speak—that is, 2008), I was approached by Cognella Academic Publishing about developing a new text for courses on the anthropology of religion, magic, and witchcraft. At that time, my first thought was that the last thing a saturated textbook market needed was yet another volume for undergraduates to wade through. As I began to consider the matter more closely, however, it dawned on me that there were still many facets of religion, the supernatural, the occult, and the paranormal in the United States and elsewhere that had yet to be mined for publication. To judge from the many news articles, journal investigations, and editorials (more online than in print, these days), ideas about an alternate universe, reality, or dimension (you choose the term!) continued to have significance in everyday American life. Claims to visions, revelations, experiences, and encounters could be found everywhere—even as the death knell of "religion" and "faith" were being sounded from various quarters. Clearly, something was being missed by perfunctory conclusions that a post-religious age was dawning in the United States.

As I began to consider the first edition of this text, I rummaged through a filing cabinet drawer in my university office, overflowing with photocopied articles and printed internet news reports about religion and religious phenomena. For some years, I had been collecting these in order to (one day) rifle through them, on the hunt for new material and "real-world" examples that might be insinuated into my courses. Even when I found no way to incorporate them into my lecture notes, for some period of time these articles—with such sensationalist titles as "Catholic Bishops: More Exorcists Needed" and "Mob Kills Witchcraft Couple"—would be tacked to a small notice board on the wall outside my office door. For my efforts, I have occasionally been rewarded with a student comment or email about these articles, and I have often been surprised by the ways in which various newsworthy events have tapped into the imaginations of students with little prior exposure. Some dozen years later, I found myself again "rummaging" for newsworthy items—this time from entirely online sources. Once again, I discovered a trove of fascinating stories, anecdotes, and analyses—many of which have made their way into these pages.

To return to the status of religion in US society, we can echo philosopher Marshall McLuhan, who famously quipped that "the medium is the message." It may be true that some parts of the world and some segments of US society are entering a post-religious age of sorts, but—as I pointed out previously—you would never know it from the vast body of descriptive and entertainment-oriented writing about the mysterious domain of the supernatural that saturates contemporary media. In this book, I am obviously dealing solely with the written word. Were I to expand this book to sample *all forms* of media that Americans are familiar with, I would need to include a tablet with purchase so that readers could watch and listen to (as well as read) some of these expressions of pop-cultural interest. If there is anything to notions of supply and demand, then surely there must be an ongoing interest among the nonspecialist and even nonchurchgoing public in those anecdotal traces of religion and the supernatural that saturate today's media. The perennial popularity of mainstream films and television shows that exploit these in the interests of popular entertainment and advertising revenue lends still more support to the idea that many Americans (and almost certainly others) are shifting away from an attitude of fidelity and respect for religion and toward one of persistent curiosity about the paranormal. While it is clear that many millions of Americans continue to anchor their sense of self and cultural identity in religion, this level of commitment can no longer be taken for granted. Even when millennials and "Gen Y" youth seek out religious experience in earnest, it is seldom with the sectarian or doctrinal leanings of their grandparents. Like it or not, the attitude toward religion is changing in this country, and only time will tell whether the many institutions of our religious culture will be reinvigorated in the new millennium. Again, it's important to point out that we seem to have entered an era that is increasingly "de-churched," a time in which fragments of belief, tradition, and practice are variously embraced, discarded, or swapped out for one another in a free marketplace of religious ideas and possibilities. The prospects for innovation spawned by the new, media-driven culture around us seem to drive, rather than destroy, ongoing interest in religion in the modern United States.

Moreover, there is another sense in which religion is not disappearing from public life. Decades ago, sociologist Robert Bellah wrote of the emergence of a late-modern world in which a large variety of civic and cultural institutions were effectively meeting the social and psychological needs and purposes of religion without actually being religious, as the word is normally construed. Thus, nation-states, professional sports, and a host of cultural associations of one kind or another all embrace and embody rituals, values, and institutions that in a very real sense "are" religion(s). Perhaps better than any other example, the nation as an "imagined community" (to use anthropologist Benedict Anderson's phrase) incorporates a wider variety of values, creeds, meanings, rituals, commitments, symbols, heroes, organizations, and roles that resemble religion—all without the apparent centrality of a creator God (although this has always been the subject of much dispute and controversy). What is the general presidential election if not the central collective ritual of the nation, observed at prescribed intervals and laden with pomp and ceremony? What are congressmen and senators if not the chief priests of the state? What are the Declaration of Independence and US Constitution if not the scriptures of the nation? And who are George Washington, Abraham Lincoln, and Martin Luther King Jr. if not the eternal heroes of the nation (much like saints in Christianity)? More prosaically, consider the vast armies of *Star Trek* and anime fans who routinely dress in costume; gather at national and international conferences; devour publications, films, and television series; and generally inhabit a world of signification that overlaps but is not isomorphic with broader US and global societies. For any probing analysis of US society, these examples are important—they point to the way in which religion must be thought of as a set of social processes and activities that are collectively much greater than the narrow definition we usually give it. Whether or not their authors have thought through these issues is, in a sense, beside the point. The many articles published on the topics of religion, the occult (a term widely used to describe secretive supernatural events, actions, and institutions), and the paranormal (another popular umbrella term generally used to describe transcendent phenomena without reference to religion) are responding to a public hunger that seems never quite satiated. It is in exploration of this craving through an anthropological lens that I devote the third edition of *Magic, Witchcraft, and Religion: Perspectives in the Media*.

As with the articles included in earlier editions, I admit to having little method in deciding which to use in this edition other than a dogged determination to keep things interesting and fresh. I discovered most through many hours of online subject searches and perusal of various websites, not to mention the vast Cognella research library, and have included only a fraction of those articles I found suitable to my purpose. I make no secret of the fact that these articles were chosen in the first instance because they fit my personal and pedagogical interests and not because I had in mind a well-rounded reader in which many religious traditions were represented. Of the 25 selections, for instance, science and the supernatural, vampires, ghosts, zombies, magic, and Satanism receive their fair share of attention, while there is little or no mention of the global traditions of Islam, Hinduism, Native American religion, Taoism, and so on. Some might consider the absence of these a large oversight, but I do not claim to be comprehensive in the general sense of that word. In theory, I could go on indefinitely adding article upon article to subsequent editions. But to do so would be impractical in terms both of length and cost.

Another goal of this third edition is to introduce students to important themes in the anthropology of religion by grouping these articles into categories, which I have reorganized since the previous edition. Each reflects a common theme that I have found useful in teaching, and various articles from earlier editions have been eliminated to make room for new ones. As in earlier editions, each part is prefaced by a discussion of the overall significance of the events, persons, and circumstances elaborated on in the articles. It has been my intention to write each of these pieces in a conversational tone and without the many academic citations, independent clauses, caveats, footnotes, and other signs of academic enterprise. As with the earlier editions, my hope for this edition is that the relative informality of my approach will prove appealing both to instructors and students, many of whom are accustomed to more ponderous, albeit more sophisticated, textbooks and readers.

Completion of this reader has not been a solitary undertaking, and I must thank Kaela Martin, Celeste Paed, Jessie Chase, Carrie Montoya, Jess Wright, Jamie Gigante, Jeanine Rees, Dani Skeen, Arek Arechiga, and all the editorial and production staff at Cognella Academic Publishing for their hard work on this third edition. I am also very grateful to the many journalists, editorialists, and production staff of the various media outlets who have supplied the "grist" for my mill. A special note of thanks is due to Benjamin Radford, who has kindly donated a brand-new article for this edition. This book is dedicated with fondness and gratitude to the many students, past and present, who have taken my course, Anthropology 13: Magic, Witchcraft, and Religion, which I have taught since 2002 at California State University, Sacramento. Over the years, they have given me the priceless opportunity to broaden my own horizons in the interests of teaching general education—for this, I cannot thank them enough.

Liam D. Murphy
May 2021

Further Readings

Anderson, Benedict. *Imagined Communities: Reflections on the Origins and Spread of Nationalism*. Rev. ed. London: Verso, 2006.

A now-classic exposition of how the origins of national consciousness and community are rooted in literacy, changes to official religion, and the global spread of empires since the fifteenth century.

Bellah, Robert N. *The Broken Covenant: American Civil Religion in Time of Trial*. 2nd ed. Chicago: University of Chicago Press, 1992.

In this work, Bellah, a renowned sociologist of religion, discusses how the institutions, values, and perspectives embedded in US civil society mirror many aspects of "traditional" US religion.

Bruce, Steve. *God Is Dead: Secularization in the West*. Chichester, UK: Wiley-Blackwell Press, 2002.

This book outlines Bruce's perspective that various events and processes (especially the popularity of Eastern and "new" religions, political scandals, and the advances of science) are now undermining the traditional authority and status of Euro-American Christianity in the twenty-first century.

Reed, Randall, and G. Michael Zbaraschuk, eds. *The Emerging Church, Millennials, and Religion, Volume 1: Prospects and Problems*. Eugene, Oregon: Cascade Books, 2018.

Essays in this edited, multidisciplinary volume explore contemporary religion through the lens of the millennial generation. In particular, contributors identify and discuss nontraditional, "post-Church" forms of religious practice currently taking shape in the United States.

A Note to Instructors

|||||||||||||||||||||||||||||||||||||||||||||||||||||||||||||||||||||||||||||||||||||||||||||||||||||||||||||||||||||||||||||||||||||||||||||||||||||||||||

The editorial text and articles contained in *Magic, Witchcraft, and Religion: Perspectives in the Media*, third edition, are written in an accessible manner that should appeal to nonanthropology majors and an educated public. Still, the volume is intended to be used in conjunction with other course materials and texts in the context of classroom instruction. Along these lines, I believe that students taking introductory and general education courses in the anthropology of religion will benefit more from the volume if they are familiar with some of the key concepts of social and cultural anthropology (for instance, culture, ritual, relativism, and ethnocentrism, as these have been defined by anthropologists). In addition, it would be of some help (but not indispensable) for students enrolled in these courses to have some general knowledge of the colonial foundations of anthropology as a discipline, together with some vantage on how non-"Western" peoples have been viewed, historically, by Europeans and European diasporas. Instructors will also note that in my part introductions, I have largely avoided lengthy digressions into anthropological theory and the "canon" of scholars generally discussed in anthropology of religion classes. *Mostly* absent is a discussion of such luminaries as E. B. Tylor, James Frazer, Bronislaw Malinowski, E. E. Evans-Pritchard, Émile Durkheim, Max Weber, and Anthony Wallace. The work of these and many others is largely (though not completely) implicit in my introductory discussions—each of which is intended to expose "classic" observations while avoiding the minutiae of theory. To reiterate, ideally, these introductions will supplement, rather than replace, a traditional textbook on the subject.

Finally, it is my hope and intention that the articles presented here provide a focus for vibrant classroom discussion. To this end, I have included a series of discussion questions and revised and annotated further readings at the conclusion of each part. Admittedly, there is little rigorous method to which works were selected for inclusion in the further readings, but I have both suggested supplementary texts by any researchers mentioned in the introductions and endeavored to present something of a mix of academic and popular material.

Introduction to the Third Edition

||||||||||||||||||||||||||||||||||||||||||||||||||||||||||||||||||||||||||||||||||||||||||||||||||||||||||||||||||||||||||||||

T he power and influence of religion in shaping US history cannot be
understated. From the earliest days of settlement by Puritans and other
"nonconformists" to the deism and freemasonry of eighteenth-century elites
(among them several "founding fathers"), to the powerful currents of African
religion kept alive throughout long years of slavery, to the influx of Catholic
and Jewish Europeans in the nineteenth century and from other parts of
the world in the twentieth and twenty-first (all of whom brought their own
distinctive ethnic and religious traditions with them), and to the efflorescence
of "new religions" and fascination with the so-called paranormal that has
emerged over the volatile decades since the end of the Second World War,
the United States has at once treasured and kept at arm's length its religious
heritage. The First Amendment of the Constitution enshrines the idea that
the government should not "establish" (that is, it should refrain from making
official) one form of religion to the subordination or exclusion of others, and
this is commonly viewed as one of the cornerstones of American "freedom."
Perhaps for this reason, there currently exists an extravagantly rich tapestry of
faith worlds and practices considered by many to be a hallmark of American
national culture. The articles throughout this volume illuminate some aspects
of how religious ideas and experience thrive at the margins of public discourse. Mediated by popular writing published across the print and electronic
media, shadows of the continuing fascination with "otherworldly" beings
and powers generally lurk in those areas of news websites and social media
devoted to entertainment, travel, popular culture, and other "less important"
stories and reportage. Unless concerned with the doings and personages of
global religious traditions, such phenomena as ghost sightings, unearthing

of vampires, and modern witchcraft may intrigue and amuse—but they are very easily dismissed by the educated public as frivolous or trivial.

To tell the story of religion in America, media coverage of events, personalities, and institutions associated with the occult, paranormal, or just plain strange often waits on dramatic developments (a court case over religious freedom or the doings of an unconventional religious group) rather than on subtle changes or everyday activities. For instance, the author has been called on at various points to shed light on such mysterious phenomena as "weeping statues" and ghost hunting, to forecast developments in the Catholic Church following the death of a beloved pope, to discuss the significance of Halloween ritual in modern society, and to identify the origin of Easter eggs. This eclectic laundry list reflects a mercurial public interest in religion and *transcendent* phenomena—at least to the extent that these (the interests and the phenomena) evolve in new, thought-provoking, and, apparently, unpredictable ways.

How should we address a fascination that seems to defy traditional expectations of religious commitment by embracing a wide diversity of issues and interests, current and historical? The word *transcendent* is useful in this discussion because it points to a world of public interest that goes beyond well-circumscribed faith worlds per se; it indicates a widespread anticipation of, and intense curiosity about, the possibilities of existence outside the world of the everyday senses—a universe that literally merges with and transcends our own without being identical to it. Other terms might be used instead (among them, supernatural, spiritual, and paranormal), but most of these carry a certain amount of cultural baggage in already being connected to well-defined sets of beliefs. The term "supernatural," for example, has been somewhat burdened by connotations of the primitive, superstitious, and illogical. The word transcendent is to this point not burdened by such expectations, and so is more useful for academic analysis. Many millions of Americans profess fascination with that which evokes or celebrates the transcendent (vampires, ghosts, and Halloween, for example) even when the thought of worshiping in a church makes them cringe. One need not be a professional student of the American landscape of religion to notice that its diversity is not fixed but is rather "on the move," with new ideas, rituals, and "traditions" coming into existence seemingly overnight and others disappearing just as quickly. There are potentially many patterns to be identified in this shifting vista of beliefs and institutions, but among the most significant are those that denote fundamental changes in how Americans perceive the role, status, and relevancy of a transcendent world in relation to human society.

This brings us to an important point. As useful as the term transcendent is, we cannot avoid the issue of what we mean by the term "religion." How should we define the word in a way that is broad enough to encompass the many ideas we pack inside it? In teaching, I have often felt that I spend more time than necessary sifting through the various possible ways to untie the knot of religion, examining it from many angles: social, historical, cultural, political, psychological, and archaeological. The simple truth is that there is no universally accepted definition of religion, if for no other reason than because for many, many people, religion is synonymous with their most intimate assumptions about ultimate, universal reality. Put another way, for the faithful, religion is not a belief system, historical epoch, or cultural construct—it is simply the truth ... notwithstanding that there are many other people who have failed to embrace it.

For my purposes in this volume, however, and because I am a social scientist, I will treat religion as a social, cultural, and historical phenomenon. More specifically, we may define as *religious* (as opposed to transcendent, which as I'm using it here refers explicitly to that alternate domain of power, value, and meaning existing "outside" the material universe) any social institution that features some or all of the following characteristics:

- recognition and/or veneration of transcendent beings, powers, and/ or principles;

- prescription of social and personal conventions, activities, and rituals that engage these transcendent beings, powers, and/or principles;

- veneration of narratives that describe the transcendent world and the place of humankind in relation to it;

- acceptance of values, dispositions, and subjective states that are appropriate and meaningful in the context of human relations with the transcendent world; or

- institutionalization and regulation of social relationships, hierarchies, and roles with the goal of sustaining and enhancing connections between humanity and the transcendent world.

All the articles presented here address some aspect of the transcendent, and most address some aspect of religion. This includes people, events, and concepts behind the terms "magic" and "witchcraft"—themselves the focus of much definitional wrangling (each of which will be defined in their part introductions). Again, remember that the word transcendent is intended to evoke the idea of a world, reality, or dimension of existence that is conjoined with, but somehow different than, our own.

Bearing in mind these open-ended definitions, one might correctly infer that it is easy to talk at cross purposes when discussing transcendent and religious phenomena—easy to assume that we're speaking of the same thing, even when I have ritual practices in mind (that is, those shared, patterned activities involving extensive manipulation of symbols and performed at specific intervals) while the person I'm conversing with is thinking that religion is about belief in God or fear of ghosts. Still, this complexity is perhaps inevitable given the plurality of our overall culture and conditions in the modern world more broadly. In the increasingly cosmopolitan society of twenty-first-century America, religious and cultural pluralism are not only valued in and of themselves but also function as a sort of ideological buffet. In ever-increasing numbers, Americans feel at liberty to explore different possibilities, indulge in new perspectives, and even cobble together their own visions of the universe based on an *à la carte* philosophy. In other words, what I mean by the term "religion" might well change over time based on my experience of the expanding social diversity all around us. So, while today I consider religion to be about institutions and practices that orient to the transcendent, who's to say that in 50 years the word will only refer to sensory experiences of a paranormal character? The term is fluid, and we, as a society, are as well.

Often, this is a net positive. In teaching, I try across all my classes to strike a sanguine tone about how useful and enriching it is to be exposed to ways of knowing, thinking, and behaving that are unlike one's own and to imagine ways in which those terms we assume to refer to permanent phenomena (like churches and creeds) may change to encompass new aspects of the transcendent. I would, however, be less than candid if I didn't point out that this strength is also a liability. Among the most problematic aspects of religion is its tendency to serve as an important barometer of social difference. Too often, the loftier, nobler goal of reuniting human beings with ultimate truth and purpose (the conceptual foundation of the word "religion"; Latin: *re-ligio*: to "re-connect") is supplanted with concerns of a more worldly nature and our baser drives: xenophobia, racism, sexism, ethnocentrism, and the intoxication of power. While denouncers of religious institutions may miss some of the more subtle beauties, ethics, joys, and profundities of commitment to a church or similar organization, they generally get it right when it comes to issues of corruption and moral hypocrisy: religion, just like all human institutions, beliefs, and practices, is prone to misuse. Moreover, because many religious worldviews distinguish the right from the wrong and the good from the evil, they very readily avail themselves of cultural processes of "othering." That is, religion is useful in the erection and support of "us versus them" forms of understanding around the world. This is especially the case when one's own cultural biases remain implicit when characterizing someone else's religion.

On this cautionary note, let us move now to the five parts in which slender slivers of print and online media attention to these themes are explored. While many of the articles subsumed within these parts touch on the same issues, each reflects a particular perspective that is useful to consider through an anthropological lens.

Further Readings

Asad, Talal. *Genealogies of Religion: Discipline and Reasons of Power in Christianity and Islam*. Baltimore: John Hopkins University Press, 1993.

A collection of well-known anthropologist Asad's essays on (primarily) Western religion and culture, including his famous response to Clifford Geertz's position on religion as a web of socially unifying symbols. Asad's general perspective is that the social, political, and economic conditions of the historical epoch "modernity" have ultimately defined what it means to have religion and be religious in Western societies.

Davies, Owen. *America Bewitched: The Story of Witchcraft After Salem*. New York: Oxford University Press, 2013.

A noted historian of Anglo-American witchcraft, Davies provides a wide-ranging look at post-Salem perspectives on and episodes of witchcraft and witchcraft persecution—especially those relating to Native Americans, African Americans, and various immigrant communities.

Émile Durkheim. *Elementary Forms of the Religious Life*. Oxford Classics. Oxford: Oxford University Press, 2008.

Durkheim's *Elementary Forms* is among a handful of foundational texts in the sociological and anthropological study of religion. In it, he marshals ethnographic examples from a host of contexts to build his case that religion is cultivated through a profound experience of collective social performance and the effervescent sense of the "sacred" that collective ritual generates.

Goldstein, Diane, Sylvia Grider, and Jeannie Banks Thomas. *Haunting Experiences: Ghosts in Contemporary Folklore*. Logan, Utah: Utah State University Press, 2007.

In this social and cultural analysis of ghost and haunting experiences and narratives, the authors look at the ways in which such claims to extraordinary encounters create and commodify various aspects of popular culture.

Marsden, George M. *Fundamentalism and American Culture*. Oxford: Oxford University Press, 2006.

Marsden offers a rich exploration of the theology, history, and influence of the Christian fundamentalist movement in US society. This work will be of special interest to students seeking to understand the role of conservative religious beliefs and institutions in twenty-first-century America.

Torrey, E. Fuller. *Evolving Brains, Emerging Gods: Early Humans and the Origins of Religion*. New York: Columbia University Press, 2019.

A contemporary analysis of the neurological, evolutionary, primatological, and archaeological basis for and theory behind religious experience and emergence of gods and spirits in human prehistory.

Part I

||||||||||||||||||||||||||||||||||||||||||||||||||||||||||||||||||||||||||||||||||||||||||||||||||||||||||||||||||||||||||||||||

Religious Fragments

Introduction

As the world becomes more tightly knit by way of mass media and communications, digital technologies, rapid travel, and the innumerable intercultural
encounters these bring, it is perhaps inevitable that very different sets of cultural
values and meanings come into conflict with one another. With the possible
exception of language, nowhere is this more apparent than in the domain of
religion, which people tend to have very strong commitments to or opinions
about. In the United States, we often assume that religious faith and acceptance of transcendent powers and beings are a matter of personal choice. In
the twenty-first century, Americans are more willing to consider and recon-
sider their religious affiliations time and again, flitting among and flirting with
options that seem more appealing at different stages of the life cycle.

Most of us would recognize that however laudable this ideal, it appears to
be observed more in the breach than in the practice. In fact, social life in the
United States and elsewhere is rife with disagreements that seem always poised
to flare into controversies of national and international import. As the articles in
Part One demonstrate, controversies have erupted over the status of explicitly
religious symbols in the public sphere—particularly in classrooms and other
state-run institutions. Debate over the morality and legality of abortion is a
perennial reminder of how deeply religion can penetrate national politics by
way of the so-called culture wars. Recent years have also witnessed sharp differences in religious conviction sparked by issues ranging from birth control to
gay marriage to euthanasia to the content of middle and high school textbooks.
From his deathbed, a Catholic cardinal prodded the Church to recommit itself

to meeting these and other challenges posed by the contemporary world. "Why don't we rouse ourselves—are we afraid?" he warns. Is more religion (or at least more faith) the answer to devastating social ills like mass shootings (as pundit Mike Huckabee warns), or has religion been a root problem in the making of a "more perfect union"? However one considers these questions, more than traditional religion is at stake in the splintering of modern faith worlds. As another of the Part One articles shows, even atheist churches have their own inner tensions and disagreements to resolve.

Such disputes have been especially heated where matters of national security are perceived to be at stake. Acrimonious debate also attended the erection of an Islamic center and mosque several city blocks away from ground zero in New York City—site of the September 11, 2001, attacks and considered by many New Yorkers and others to be sacred ground. This particular controversy took a still more bizarre turn when, in July 2010, a Floridian evangelical pastor, Terry Jones, made public his intentions to stage a Quran burning on the grounds of his small church in Gainesville—an event Jones asserted could only be derailed by a change in plans regarding the location of the center. Ultimately, the mosque and community center were indeed opened in 2011, only for the developer to petition in 2014 for a right to demolish and redevelop the property for a new Islamic museum on the same site.

Perhaps the most interesting feature of the Terry Jones episode (which ended when Jones unceremoniously announced that God had called upon him to change his mind) was how quickly this local incident became an international conflagration, with senior military and political figures warning of retaliation against US troops stationed abroad and foreign leaders and diplomats calling for federal intervention. This explosion of interest may have been exacerbated by mainstream media, but it was almost certainly fanned by online communities and bloggers focusing a spotlight on what might otherwise have proved an obscure act. Such is the power of modern digital communications that words, sounds, and images collected in one place are instantaneously available to others across the street or around the world. In light of their continuing power to influence perception and value, religion and transcendent beliefs become foci for disagreement in a way that would have been impossible even a generation ago. As late as the 1980s, it was possible for a discrete request made to a senior newspaper or media editor to prevent knowledge of certain events from being released. In the past 20 years, our understanding of what "gatekeepers" are has been radically transformed to the point where it is difficult even to identify any. In this age of the 24-hour cable news cycle, fueled by leagues of i-Reporters and citizen journalists, we should only expect ever-deeper fault lines to appear and chasms to open in which faith is pitted against faith and religion against the state.

This first part presents a collection of articles that illuminate not only the way in which such conflicts have unfolded but also the general confusion, head-scratching, and apparent bafflement that often accompanies them. Considering the scope of these articles, it is fair to say that many in the United States and elsewhere tend to esteem religion and transcendent phenomena without necessarily knowing a great deal about the historical and cultural foundations for any practice or institution in particular. Articles presented in this part all raise important questions concerning the status of religion and religious change in the twenty-first century. What does religion mean for Americans and other Westerners living in a time of cultural and religious plurality? How do a person's age and life position affect adherence to religion? Is it possible to sustain spirituality and faith in the absence of institutional religion? What are the potential consequences for a society that ignores traditional institutions of faith?

It is hoped that questions such as these will provide grist for lively classroom conversation and debate about where all things religious and supernatural stand in the uncharted waters of twenty-first-century America.

Reading 1.1

What Americans Know About Religion

By Pew Research Center

> *U.S. adults generally can answer basic questions about the Bible and Christianity, but are less familiar with other world religions.*

[...]

T HE SURVEY FINDS THAT AMERICANS' LEVELS of religious knowledge vary depending not only on what questions are being asked, but also on who is answering. Jews, atheists, agnostics and evangelical Protestants, as well as highly educated people and those who have religiously diverse social networks, show higher levels of religious knowledge, while young adults and racial and ethnic minorities tend to know somewhat less about religion than the average respondent does.

Most Americans correctly answer basic questions about Christianity, atheism and Islam; fewer know about Judaism, Hinduism or what the Constitution says

% who answer each question correctly

87%
What is an atheist?

A. Someone who believes in God
B. Does NOT believe in God
C. Is unsure whether God exists
D. Believes in multiple gods

81%
What is commemorated on Easter Sunday?

A. Resurrection
B. Ascension
C. Crucifixion
D. Last Supper

60%
What is Ramadan?

A. Hindu festival of lights
B. Jewish prayer for the dead
C. An Islamic holy month
D. Festival celebrating Buddha's birth

27%
What does the U.S. Constitution say about religion as it relates to federal officeholders?

A. No religious test shall be necessary for holding office
B. They shall be sworn in using the Holy Bible
C. They shall affirm all men are endowed by their Creator with unalienable rights
D. Nothing

19%
How many adults in the U.S. are Jewish?

A. Less than 5%
B. About one-in-ten
C. About one-in-four
D. Half or more

15%
Which text is most closely associated with Hinduism?

A. Tao Te Ching
B. Vedas
C. Quran
D. Mahayana sutras

Note: Correct answers are highlighted. For most survey questions, the order in which the answers were listed was randomized. Respondents had the option to click "not sure" on all questions. See topline for full question wording and order.
Source: Survey conducted Feb. 4-19, 2019, among U.S. adults.
"What Americans Know About Religion"

PEW RESEARCH CENTER

Overall, eight-in-ten U.S. adults correctly answer that in the Christian tradition, Easter commemorates the *resurrection* of Jesus—rather than the Crucifixion, the Ascension to heaven or the Last Supper. A similar share know that the Christian doctrine of the Trinity holds that there is one God in three persons—the Father, the Son and the Holy Spirit. Eight-in-ten Americans correctly identify Moses as the biblical figure who led the Exodus from Egypt, and David as the one who killed an enemy by slinging a stone, while seven-in-ten know that Abraham is the biblical figure who exhibited a willingness to sacrifice his son in obedience to God.

Most Americans also are familiar with two different terms that indicate a lack of belief in God. Almost nine-in-ten correctly identify the definition of "an atheist" (someone who does not believe in God), and six-in-ten correctly select the definition of "an agnostic" (someone who is unsure whether God exists).

[...]

On the other hand, Americans are less familiar with some basic facts about other world religions, including Judaism, Buddhism and Hinduism. Just three-in-ten U.S. adults know that the Jewish Sabbath begins on Friday, one-quarter know that Rosh Hashana is the Jewish New Year, and one-in-eight can correctly identify the religion of Maimonides (an influential Jewish scholar in the Middle Ages).

Roughly one-in-five Americans (18%) know that the "truth of suffering" is among Buddhism's four "noble truths," and just 15% correctly identify the Vedas as a Hindu text.

Many Americans also struggle to answer some questions about the size of religious minorities in the U.S. and about religion's role in American government. For instance, most U.S. adults overestimate the shares of Jews and Muslims in the U.S. or are unaware that Jews and Muslims each account for less than 5% of the population. And when asked what the U.S. Constitution says about religion as it relates to federal officeholders, just one-quarter (27%) correctly answer that it says "no religious test" shall be a qualification for holding office; 15% incorrectly believe the Constitution requires federal officeholders to affirm that all men are endowed by their Creator with certain unalienable rights, 12% think the Constitution requires elected officials to be sworn in using the Bible, 13% think the Constitution is silent on this issue, and 31% say they are not sure.

America Must Take a Good Look in the Mirror—and Stop the Hatred

By Armstrong Williams, Opinion Contributor

I F THERE EVER WAS A MOMENT when we Americans needed to take a good look in the mirror, it's now. When I stare at the face of America, I see a distorted image of a country needlessly plagued by hatred. It is hatred fueled by ignorant prejudices toward people of different races, religions, ethnicities and lifestyles.

The United States has stood as a beacon of diversity—a democracy that celebrates differences. This is the land where the greatest civil rights movement of all time broke the shackles of old bigotries.

That's why the recent uptick in religious and race-based hatred is so shocking and disheartening. The climate of hate seems to be worsening, spreading in alarming and tragic ways. Since the 2012 shootings at Sandy Hook Elementary School, more than 2,100 mass shootings have happened in America, and they are tearing us apart.

My own cousin, the Rev. Clementa Pickney, was just one of far too many victims. He was gunned down by a troubled young man in his church in South Carolina. After being welcomed into the house of prayer with open arms by those in attendance, the attacker then turned on them out of his hatred toward African Americans. He took lives and shattered families—for what?

The numbers show that hatred is climbing. In 2018, the Southern Poverty Law Center documented 1,020 active hate groups in the United States. That same year, the Anti-Defamation League recorded a total of 1,879 attacks against Jews and Jewish institutions in America—including the most deadly attack against the Jewish community in American history at Tree of Life synagogue in Pittsburgh.

Minority groups from coast to coast, including blacks, Muslims, Jews, non-white immigrants and the LGBTQ community, have come under attack—online, in houses of worship, in workplaces, at schools and playgrounds.

What is the driving force behind those who choose to hate others so blindly?

Recently, I interviewed a former neo-Nazi skinhead to explore the root of his hatred. This man had never met a Jewish person but vehemently hated them all. At one point, this man needed a job. Living in Philadelphia, he was given a job by a Jewish business owner who mentored him, showered him with respect and treated him with kindness. That's when the former neo-Nazi changed for the better. He realized that he had been brainwashed to hate Jews. Ignorance is one of mankind's worst enemies.

To explore the source of hatred further, I also sat down with the director of the U.S. Holocaust Memorial Museum, Sara Bloomfield, to talk about how and why anti-Semitism has existed for more than 2,000 years. She likens anti-Semitism to a cancer that finds different places to morph and manifest itself. She spoke of conspiracy theories, myths and misinformation that have been promulgated over the centuries about Jews—especially in the lands where they were persecuted as minorities and labeled as "the other."

As the director of one of America's most important institutions, which serves as a living memorial to the Holocaust and a databank of historical evidence of genocide, Bloomfield shares the heavy responsibility of imparting the lessons of the Holocaust to prevent future atrocities.

This responsibility is one that all Americans should shoulder. It is incumbent upon us not to become numb and complacent to stereotypes and hateful rhetoric, but to stand up against them and to promote diversity and human dignity.

We can, and must, do better. Regardless of our race, gender or ethnicity, we are all made in the image of our Creator. We must learn to live together and love one another.

We are supposed to be the United States of America. With this title comes our collective obligation to treat one another with civility. Our code of conduct must include respect for differences, perspectives and political views. To succeed as a nation, Americans must find a way to have civil discourse without discord.

True success will be the day when we can look at one another devoid of hatred and ignorance, and when we can look at ourselves in the mirror and be proud of the diversity we see.

Op-Ed: Mike Huckabee Ties Mass Shootings to an Absence of Faith in God. Social Science Proves Him Wrong

By Phil Zuckerman

I N THE WAKE OF YET ANOTHER *and another and another* mass shooting in America—with at least 34 dead in Gilroy, El Paso and Dayton—Mike Huckabee, the former governor turned pundit, repeated his go-to response: Gun violence in our country is all about waning belief in God.

As he piously proclaimed in a recent televised interview: "The common denominator in all of this is … disconnecting from God. … A lot of our country [is] utterly disconnected from any sense of identity with their creator." Huckabee was even more explicit after the Sandy Hook mass shooting in 2012 that killed 26, including many young children. Such violence occurs, he said, because "we have systematically removed God from our schools."

Huckabee, the former governor of Arkansas, is far from alone in holding this view. After the latest mass shootings, Texas Lt. Gov. Dan Patrick said on "Fox and Friends"that if Americans don't adequately praise God, the result will be continued carnage.

So there you have it: Mass shootings in America are the direct result of people not having enough active faith in God.

The interesting thing about this hypothesis is that it is easy to test. You've got an independent variable (faith in God) and a dependent variable (gun violence). The hypothesis put forth by Huckabee and other Christian moralizers comes down to this: When a given society has a higher amount of faith in God, the rate of gun violence should be correspondingly lower. Conversely, the lower the amount of faith in God, the higher the rate of gun violence.

But social science finds the exact opposite correlation.

The facts show that strong faith in God does not diminish gun violence, nor does a lack of such faith increase gun violence.

Here's one crystal-clear example: Faith in God is extremely high in the Philippines. One study found that the country "leads the world" in terms of its strength of faith in God, with 94% of people there saying they have always believed in God. Comparatively, the Czech Republic, is one of the most atheistic nations in the world, with only about 20% of Czechs believing in God. According to Huckabee's hypothesis, violence and murder rates should be much worse in the Czech Republic and much better in the Philippines.

But the reality is different: The murder rate in the Philippines is nearly 10 times higher than it is in the Czech Republic, according to the United Nations Office on Drugs and Crime.

This same correlation holds true for nearly every country in the world: Those with the strongest rates of belief in God—such as El Salvador, Columbia, Honduras, Jamaica, and Yemen—tend to experience the most violence, while those with the lowest rates— such as Japan, Sweden, the Netherlands, Finland, New Zealand and Australia—tend to experience the lowest levels of violence.

Are there exceptions? Yes. For example, New Zealand experienced a horrific mass shooting in March. Norway did as well, in 2011. But when looking at averages and correlations over time, the statistical relationship they reveal is unambiguous: Huckabee's hypothesis doesn't hold water.

By any standard measure, the safest countries in the world are highly secularized nations like Iceland, Denmark, Canada, Slovenia and South Korea—where faith in God is very low. And the most dangerous countries include fervently faithful places such as the Central African Republic, Syria, Sudan, Venezuela and Belize—places steeped in faith in God.

But the analysis can also be applied closer to home, to the 50 states. According to the Pew Religious Landscape survey, the states with the strongest levels of faith in God include Louisiana, Arkansas, Alabama, Mississippi, Georgia, South Carolina, North Carolina, Kentucky, Tennessee and Oklahoma. Those with the lowest levels of belief in God are Maine, Vermont, Connecticut, New Hampshire, Rhode Island, Massachusetts, New York, Alaska, Oregon and California. And, as expected, when it comes to homicide rates and violent crime rates in general, the least faithful states in America tend to experience far less than the most faithful.

Of course, there are many different reasons that some nations—or states—have higher rates of violence. For instance, higher rates of gun ownership have been tied to higher rates of domestic homicides. Factors like economics, politics, culture and a host of other aspects of social life also play their part.

But that's the point. People's relationship with the divine doesn't have much, if anything, to do with it. Huckabee's hypothesis needs to be rejected not only because it is statistically incorrect, but because it's also inhumane: By blaming mass shootings on a lack of God-worship, he is implicitly asserting that the many victims of gun violence, well, *deserved* it.

On average, about 13,000 Americans are killed by guns every year. And every day, approximately seven children are killed by guns. Such endless carnage and horror will only stop with sane laws and ethical policies.

Faith in God will do nothing to end the epidemic of mass shootings in America, save perhaps to serve as a balm for the souls of the many Americans forced to weep at funerals for victims of gun violence.

Reading 1.4

Is It Time for the U.S. Church to Hold a Regional Synod to Address the Abuse Crisis?

By Russell Shaw

WASHINGTON (CNS)—THE CONFERENCE OF BISHOPS, meeting in Dallas, had lately adopted a charter and norms for the protection of children. Now the eight called for something more. Convene a plenary council or regional synod, they urged their fellow bishops, and use it to get at the roots of what had happened so as to prevent anything like that from ever happening again. The signers of their joint letter included Cardinal Daniel N. DiNardo of Galveston-Houston, then bishop of Sioux City, Iowa, and now president of the national bishops' conference, and Archbishop Allen H. Vigneron of Detroit, an auxiliary bishop there back then.

More than a hundred bishops expressed interest in the suggestion, which eventually came to focus on the synod option. The bishops' conference took some note of it. But in time, enthusiasm faded and the proposal died as the hierarchy went about implementing their new child protection measures.

Now it seems that those eight bishops were ahead of their time. In the face of a crisis even worse than 17 years ago, the idea of a regional synod for the Catholic Church in the United States looks increasingly appealing.

"In the long experience of the church," the eight bishops told their brother bishops in 2002, "the taking of action by bishops through a council or synod has been a tried and true strategy to advance reform." And most people would agree that there's a need for church reform now.

The crisis has grown and now no longer involves only the sexual abuse of children by some clerics. Instead it has become a crisis of ecclesial communion whose elements include mistrust of church leaders heightened by the McCarrick and Bransfield affairs, tension and conflict among ideologically motivated groups all claiming they represent authentic Catholicism, and a dismaying gulf between what the church teaches and what many Catholics believe on both faith and morals.

Numbers underline the seriousness of the situation. Last year, there were 143,000 Catholic marriages in the United States compared with more than 426,000 in 1970. Infant baptisms numbered 615,000 as against 1.089 million back then. The percentage of Catholics attending Mass weekly fell from 54.9% in 1970 to 21.1% in 2018. Half the Catholics age 30 and younger have left the church, while, as Auxiliary Bishop Robert E. Barron of Los Angeles points out, for every person who joins the church today, six leave.

Against this background, an appropriate theme for a regional synod might be "The Challenge of Transmitting the Faith."

The Code of Canon Law speaks of regional synods as "special sessions" whose members are the bishops of the region involved or bishops chosen to represent them. Since the Second Vatican Council there have been regional synods for the Netherlands, Lebanon, Africa, the Middle East, and other places. A regional synod for the Amazon region of Latin America will be held in October.

In his address to the bishops at their general meeting in Baltimore last June—read for him by one of his staff because he was in Rome attending a meeting convened by Pope Francis—Archbishop Christophe Pierre, papal nuncio to the U.S., seemed to make the case for a regional synod.

Speaking of the need for bishops to collaborate on solving problems, he said, "Personally, I believe that the body of bishops is stronger and more effective working together and walking together. Since the beginning of his pontificate Pope Francis has called for a synodal church—a church that walks together."

And he added, "In the process of walking together, we also have the opportunity to hear the different members of the group. Certainly, the church needs to listen to the voices and insights of the lay faithful. … A bishop cannot think that matters concerning the church can be resolved by acting alone or exclusively among peers."

But, someone might ask, how could a regional synod of bishops possibly be anything except bishops acting "exclusively among peers"? The answer seems obvious. The synod should be preceded by a serious, honest consultation of Catholics to find out how they see the present crisis—input of the utmost importance in shaping a realistic agenda for the synod. And beyond consultation, laypeople should be present at the synod itself as observers with the right to speak.

Certainly there are risks, particularly the risk of disappointed expectations if the pre-synod consultation appeared to be mainly for show or if the synod itself wasn't fully transparent or produced only negligible results.

But a well-planned and well-executed regional synod also offers important advantages arguably available now in no other way. Most of all, it would give the bishops an opportunity to refurbish their credibility as effective leaders while giving other Catholics reason to think their voices are being heard and reason to hope for real reform.

"In the revelation of Jesus Christ we have all the resources we need to transform this time of trial into a 'day the Lord has made,'" the eight bishops said back in 2002. "We must witness with all the authority of our apostolic ministry to bedrock Gospel principles, and we must chart a course of action on the basis of these principles."

That's at least as true now as it was then. A regional synod for the church in the United States is one way—maybe the best way and possibly the only way—to get it done.

Atheist Church Split: Sunday Assembly and Godless Revival's "Denominational Chasm"

By The Huffington Post

T HOUGH THE SUNDAY ASSEMBLY "ATHEIST CHURCH" was founded just last year by comedians Pippa Evans and Sanderson Jones, it expanded quickly from just one London congregation to 28 in cities around the world. Perhaps then, it isn't so surpris-

ing that its dynamism has now led to a schism within the newly minted group.

A blog post by Lee Moore, a founder of The Godless Revival, titled, "The Sunday Assembly has a Problem with Atheism," outlined the issues that led to the break.

He said that he initially volunteered with Sunday Assembly NYC after Sanderson Jones brought his movement to the United States, becoming an organizing member who helped determine the U.S. branch's future after Jones left. Moore explained, "A minority of organizers wished to make the event not a show but an actual church service and agreed with Jones about cutting out the word Atheist, not having speakers from the Atheist community, avoiding having an Atheist audience, and moving the show out of a bar setting to a more formal church-like setting."

CNN reports that Jones denied telling the NYC group to stop using the word "atheism," but acknowledged that he told them "not to cater solely to atheists." He also recommended choosing a more family-friendly venue rather than the dive bar where they originally gathered.

Moore alleged that after some successful events, a minority on the board which preferred not to use the word "atheist" resigned en-masse with Jones' blessing, "with the intent to turn the Sunday Assembly into something more like a Unitarian church service."

"What started out as a comedic Atheist church wants to turn itself into some sort of centralized humanist religion," he wrote, "with Sanderson Jones and Pippa Evans at the helm."

Moore didn't let his differences with Jones and Evans deter him from the overall benefit of a regular meeting for atheists, and has now founded The Godless Revival as an alternative to Sunday Assembly NYC. He announced in the blog post, "Michael Dorian, a former NYC SA board member and NY State Director for American Atheists, has teamed-up with Don Albert, another former board member and musical director for NYC SA, and myself to bring you something new. We have named this new endeavor The Godless Revival, and it will be the celebration of Atheism that you deserve."

Jones told CNN that the split was "very sad," but overall contributed to the vibrancy of the atheist community itself. He said, "Ultimately, it is for the benefit of the community. One day, I hope there will soon be communities for every different type of atheist, agnostic and humanist. We are only one flavor of ice cream, and one day we hope there'll be congregations for every godless palate."

Discussion Questions

1. How would you characterize modern US attitudes toward religion and religious organizations? How much do Americans actually know about religion, and in what ways do you think this affects their perspective on other aspects of social life (for instance non-European religious traditions and the relationship between religion and government)?

2. Based on these readings, how would you describe the role of religious intolerance in creating social division in US society? In what ways does this happen?

3. In what ways have controversies such as child sexual abuse and the proliferation of guns been addressed by religious figures and authorities? Do you believe these responses have been adequate?

4. Discuss Christian responses to atheism, both from the point of view of church clergy and the rank-and-file faithful. Which elements stand out as most important to this dispute?

5. If you had to predict the future of religion in the United States, would you anticipate a thriving and diverse assortment of faith institutions and practices? In contrast, would you view religion in steep decline, with secular-modern knowledge and values taking its place? Somewhere in between? Make the case for each of these possible outcomes.

Further Readings

Austin, Michael W. *Gods and Guns in America*. Grand Rapids: Eerdmans Publishing, 2020.

A nonpartisan analysis of the legal and ethical issues surrounding gun ownership that frames the possibilities for a robust Christian response to one of the most intractable sociopolitical issues in the modern United States.

Fletcher, Jeannine Hill. *The Sin of White Supremacy: Christianity, Racism, and Religious Diversity in America*. Maryknoll, New York: Orbis Books, 2017.

A disturbing analysis of the historical entanglements of Christian theology and racial discrimination that also offers hope for a way to transcend the dual binds of structural racism and white supremacy.

Gillis, Chester. *Roman Catholicism in America*. New York: Columbia University Press, 2000.

Gillis provides a compelling overview of the history of Catholicism in the United States and shows how late-twentieth-century American Catholics incorporate (and sometimes avoid incorporating) traditional perspectives, values, and activities into their culture of faith.

Hollinger, David A. *Protestants Abroad: How Missionaries Tried to Change the World but Changed America*. Princeton: Princeton University Press, 2017.

Hollinger provides a rich investigation of the historical and cultural world of twentieth-century Protestant missionary work abroad and critical insight into the contributions that these missionaries and their children have made to American public life.

Lewis, James R., and Jesper Aa. Petersen, eds. *Controversial New Religions.* 2nd ed. New York: Oxford University Press, 2014.

A wide-ranging sourcebook for readings on new, occult, unconventional, and controversial religions. Readings span a variety of categories of religious movements, from UFO and New Age religions to Eastern spiritualities and Western fundamentalisms.

Reitman, Janet. *Inside Scientology: The Story of America's Most Secretive Religion.* New York: Houghton Mifflin, 2011.

In this critically acclaimed work of investigative journalism, Reitman explores the details of L. Ron Hubbard's biography and the history and inner workings of the Church of Scientology as few have done before. Her exposé is among the best examinations of a new religious movement published to date.

Stephens, Mitchell. *Imagine There's No Heaven: How Atheism Helped Create the Modern World.* New York: St. Martin's Press, 2014.

This well-researched journalistic account documents the emergence and influence of atheistic philosophies from antiquity through the twenty-first century. In particular, the author shows how advances in human knowledge and ethical behavior (such as the Enlightenment, Scientific Revolution, abolitionism, and organized labor) have grown in part out of deep questioning of such concepts as God and the divine right of kings.

Stowe, David W. *No Sympathy for the Devil: Christian Pop Music and the Transformation of American Evangelicalism.* Chapel Hill: University of North Carolina Press, 2011.

Stowe explores the fast-growing world of Christian popular music in the United States, particularly with respect to the ways it has been influenced by mainstream rock music. The blossoming and popularity of Christian music reveal ways in which young people in evangelical churches respond to new social and technological circumstances in the twenty-first century and avoid the various social stigmas attached by millennials and others to traditional evangelical religion.

Part II

|||||||||||||||||||||||||||||||||||||||||||||||||||||||||||||||||||||||||||||||||||||||||||||||||||||||||||||||||||||||

Mythic Longings

Introduction

In the beginning, there were stories. The tales we tell each other; the tales we write down, narrate, make films about, etc. One thing every American can probably agree upon is that storytelling, however it is done and by whom, is vital to how people make life meaningful, entertaining, and even sublime. The very general category of "stories" is often qualified by many descriptions and adjectives, but in Standard American English, among the most common are novels, dramas, comedies, fantasies, mysteries, gospels, fairy tales, and so on. One that stands out, and which will be the focus of Part Two, is *myth*.

In contemporary American culture, the terms myth and mythology generally conjure one of two perspectives: first, many believe these terms refer to stories or ideas that are primitive, mistaken, fictional, and false and, second (in a related, if more charitable sense), that they describe fantasy worlds, characters, and narratives that are essentially make-believe but may, in some cases, serve as allegories for events in the "real" world. Both understandings depend upon an underlying assumption that is the inverse of the one used in scholarship—that myths are poetic narratives, not descriptive ones; that they express subjective and emotional perspectives, not objective and rational ones and, above all, that they derive from the imagination rather than the factual. In sum, such narratives are widely considered to be "mere" fictions born of ancient or primitive culture and reasoning, the content of which cannot be taken seriously by any rational, modern intellect. It is widely accepted that the linguistic association between myths, fictions, and lies derives from the last 200 or 300 years of Western culture—a period in which rationality, objectivity, quantitative methods, and scientific knowledge have been naturalized as the most authentic and valued ways of understanding the universe. Myth, as contrasted with official religion (which continued to be authoritative and socially respected in Eurocentric societies) became increasingly associated with the ancient world, on the one hand, and the so-called primitive cultures of the non-European world on the other. It was no great leap, therefore, for the term itself to become a byword for that which is not true, real, or objective.

This historical and popular understanding contrasts dramatically (so to speak) with more technical definitions embraced by various academic disciplines—among them anthropology, classics, folklore, historical linguistics, and comparative religion. The word myth derives from the Ancient Greek *mythos*, which referred to a very specific type of narrative: one that has a "sacred" character. Sacred stories, as opposed to mundane or profane ones, are those that tie the lives of human beings to a transcendent order of existence together with all that one finds there (including gods, deities, ancestor spirits, demons, and unseen powers of many types). Depending on which branch of scholarship one consults, there are differences of approach and perspective. Folklorists, for instance, study oral and written narratives and tend to take what we may call a strict interpretation of what counts as myth. For these, myths are by definition focused on the origins of things that are important to humanity—among others, the universe, the world, animals, stars, various foodstuffs, death, fire, the sea, and, naturally, human beings themselves. Classicists and historical linguists also lean heavily toward transcendent-centered narratives, have a tradition of hewing closely to stories from ancient civilizations around the world, and depend heavily on the work of archaeologists, philologists, Assyriologists, Egyptologists, Sinologists, and a bevy of other culture-specific specialists. Sociocultural anthropologists, for their part, have tended to have a "looser" understanding of the mythological. For these, any story could be considered a myth if it expressed ideas of central value to a social community, regardless of whether they focused exclusively (or even at all) on the transcendent. Typically, an anthropological understanding of myths holds these narratives to be characterized by some or all of the following features:

- Myths are *stories that have plots and themes* (as opposed to doctrines, descriptions, creeds, liturgies, and other genres associated with the sacred).

- Myths are *timeless* or, perhaps more accurately, "outside of time." This means that the core theme of any given myth is true regardless of whether it is historically "real" in the everyday sense. As anthropologists say, these stories exist in "mythic time" rather than "chronological time"—they are, as the expression goes, "always already"—existing simultaneously in what we usually call the past, present, and future.

- Myths feature *characters* who inhabit the plot: protagonists, antagonists, zoomorphic beings (which blend animal and human features), demigods, archetypical figures (the virgin, the hero, the crone, the fool, and so on). While divine beings may be involved (and often are), they are not indispensable to an anthropological definition of myth—although they frequently make for a better story!

- Myths are *not* associated with an author or authors. Circulating socially without a distinctive point of origin, their lack of origin contributes to a sense of their permanence and eternal nature. In this way, they contrast with such genres as novels, prophecies, and revelations.

- Myths as stories are not simply "known." Rather, for a myth to be a myth, it has to be the object of deep beliefs, motivations, and emotional commitments within a social community. Examples of this include the Christian nativity story, origin of the universe, as told in Genesis; the night of the Buddha's awakening; the First Thanksgiving story; and elements of the Salem Witchcraft persecutions of 1692.

- Myths often (but not always) foreground the *extraordinary*—that is, events and characters that are unique (or at least rare) and "beyond" what is expected of the mundane universe. As a rule, the mythologically extraordinary can neither be confirmed nor denied as "real" or "true" in the conventional sense of those words.

- Myths generally justify, explain, or highlight existing social institutions and relationships within a social community. In so doing, they generate a "road map," as it were, or, as famous anthropologist Bronislaw Malinowski asserted, a "social charter" that provides direction for behavior and a sense of control over a capricious natural universe.

Scholarly perspectives aside, if most people agreed upon which stories were obviously "mythical" (that is, false, as opposed to a different adjective "mythic," which is often a positive valorization of a given story's power or profundity), then there might be little cause for debate or disagreement. Because there is considerable ambivalence about the meaning and historical character of many stories that *seem* mythological but that are nevertheless held to be real, true, and historical by many in the United States and elsewhere—especially those connected to faith and religion—some of these narratives provoke sharp disagreements that occasionally spill out into the popular media. The articles in this part reflect this tension. They discuss, for instance, the extent to which Americans of various backgrounds and religious affiliations navigate the tension between religion and science—a tension that often focuses on debates about the truth of religious myths. From the 1980s, for instance, Reading 2.1 discusses the ways in which old-style creationism (according to which the first chapters of Genesis were in effect the textbook for understanding human origins) has been restyled as intelligent design, and instead of rejecting scientific methods outright, more recent generations of fundamentalists have proposed that they offer a scientific alternative to Darwinian evolutionary theory. In general terms, this perspective holds that a species as gifted and complex as humans could hardly be random—the accidental product of genetic mutations interacting with an indifferent ecology. Instead, they propose that human complexity and dominance furnish evidence that we are central to God's plan for the world and that such is borne out in both the archaeological and paleoanthropological records. In other words, they place an especially meaningful sacred story at the center of science. Whether this resolution offers a productive path forward in the controversy is debatable. Intelligent design perspectives inform other aspects of US religious culture, such as the Ark Encounter discussed in Reading 2.2. Overall, advocates for this strand of religion seem determined to "double down" on biblical mythology as history. Regardless of how one feels about these and other disputes, what matters here is that the "triumph" of scientific rationalism in the twenty-first century has been overstated, to say the least.

Other articles in Part Two look at the social significance and conception of myth in broader terms. Reading 2.3 argues that a misleading and two-dimensional reading of Viking mythology has both obscured the social complexity of the medieval Norse world and assisted "Alt-Right" white supremacists in crafting a new exclusive mythology of their own. Reading 2.4 turns to mass popular culture, asking whether comic and film superheroes can truly be said to "qualify" as mythological characters when the gods and deities of traditional cosmologies generally transcend the human altogether. Rather, are these characters and the stories they inhabit "anti-myths"? As discussed previously, anthropologists might well take issue with this reduction of mythic characters to the lone attribute of godlike status. But what stands out as most interesting in all of these articles is not the problems they resolve so much as the questions they raise in media that find their way out to a broad and curious public. Finally, in Reading 2.5, twentieth-century French philosopher Jean-Paul Sartre holds up a cracked mirror to the "typical" American to show us just how riven our mythic visions have been even as long ago as the post-Second World War years. While we indulge our "craving for the marvelous by reading every day in the 'comics' the incredible adventures of Superman [sic]" even then the rupture between the stories we tell ourselves about who we are and the ways in which we actually live could not be more stark. If, as Sartre tells us of the American people, the fragmented myth of "Americanism" is "not in them, they are in it," how should Americans today understand the roles and meanings of stories that simultaneously inform, entertain, and stoke our emotions?

How Many Creationists Are There in America?

By Cary Funk, Greg Smith, and David Masci

A new survey shows the number can vary considerably depending how you ask questions about evolution.

M ORE THAN A CENTURY AND A half after Charles Darwin published his groundbreaking thesis on the development of life, evolution remains a contentious topic in the United States. Most biologists and other scientists contend that evolutionary theory convincingly explains the origins and development of life on Earth. So why are some Americans still arguing about it today?

The answer lies, in large part, in the theological implications of evolutionary thinking. For many religious people, the Darwinian view of life—a panorama of brutal struggle and constant change—may conflict with both the biblical creation story and the Judeo-Christian concept of an active, loving God who intervenes in human events.

A look back at American history shows that, in many ways, questions about evolution have served as proxies in larger debates about religious, ethical and social norms. In particular, religious concerns with evolutionary theory have driven the decades-long opposition to teaching it in public schools. Even within the last 15 years, educators, scientists, parents, religious leaders and others in more than a dozen states have engaged in public battles in school boards, legislatures and courts over how school curricula should handle evolution. These battles have ebbed in recent years, but they have not died out.

The highly charged debates over evolution make it particularly difficult to measure public views on the topic. For this reason, Pew Research Center has experimented with different ways of asking survey questions about evolution and has studied how these variations affect the public's responses.

Recently, the center conducted a survey in which respondents were randomly assigned to be asked about evolution in one of two ways.

How the single- and two-question formats of the evolution question differ

Single-question format	Two-question format
Q1 Which statement comes closest to your views?	Q2 Which statement comes closer to your views?
Humans have always existed in their present form	Humans have always existed in their present form
Humans evolved; God had a role	Humans evolved
Humans evolved; God had **no** role	Those who said "evolved" were asked about the process:
	Q2 Which statement comes closer to your views?
	God had a role
	God had **no** role

Note: See questionnaire for exact wording.

PEW RESEARCH CENTER

Half of the respondents were asked for their views using a two-question "branched choice" format. First, they were asked whether they believe that humans have always existed in their present form, or that humans have evolved over time. Then, those who said humans *have* evolved were branched to a second question, asking whether they believe that evolution occurred in a process guided or allowed by God, or that evolution occurred through processes like natural selection without involvement from God.

The other half of respondents were asked a single question about their views on evolution and given three response options: "Humans have evolved over time due to processes such as natural selection; God or a higher power had no role in this process"; "Humans have evolved over time due to processes that were guided or allowed by God or a higher power"; or "Humans have existed in their present form since the beginning of time."

Overall, the percentage of Americans who take the "creationist" position is lower in the single-question format (when survey respondents are given an immediate option to express both acceptance of evolution and belief that God or a higher power had a role in such processes) than in the two-question format. When asked the single-question version, just 18 percent of U.S adults say humans have always existed in their present form, while 81 percent say humans have evolved over time. By contrast, in the two-question approach, nearly one third of respondents (31 percent) say humans have always existed in their present form, and 68 percent say they evolved over time. These results suggest that some Americans who *do* accept that humans have evolved are reluctant to say so in the two-question approach, perhaps because they are uncomfortable placing themselves on the secular side of a cultural divide.

The effect of the different question formats is especially pronounced among two of the most religious subsets of U.S. Christians: white evangelical Protestants and black Protestants. When asked using the two-question format, about two thirds of white evangelical Protestants (66 percent) take a "creationist" stance, saying that "humans have

The shares of white evangelical and black Protestants who say humans have evolved depend on how the question is asked

% of each religious group who say humans have evolved over time or existed in their present form since the beginning of time

GROUPS WHOSE RESPONSES VARY BY QUESTION FORMAT

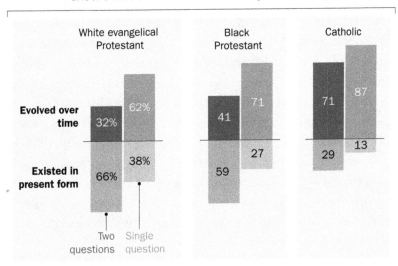

GROUPS WHOSE RESPONSES **DO NOT** VARY BY QUESTION FORMAT

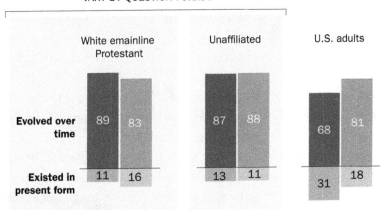

Note: Respondents who gave other responses or who did not give an answer are not shown.

Source: Survey conducted April 23–May 6, 2018.

PEW RESEARCH CENTER

always existed in their present form since the beginning of time." But when asked about human evolution in a single-question format, a 62 percent majority of white evangelical Protestants take the position that humans have evolved over time.

Similarly, 59 percent of black Protestants who were asked about this topic in the two-question format say humans have always existed in their present form. By contrast, with the single-question format, just 27 percent of black Protestants take the "creationist" position, while a 71 percent majority say humans have evolved over time.

These findings are in keeping with arguments by sociologists of religion that highly religious Americans may feel conflicted about saying humans have evolved, unless they are able to clarify that they also believe God had a hand in the development of life. Indeed, the subset of people who respond differently to the two survey approaches consists mainly of those who believe that God or a higher power played a role in human evolution. For example, nearly all white evangelical Protestants who say humans have evolved—whether in a branched-choice or single-question format—also say God had a role in human evolution.

There are smaller differences among Catholics in response to the two different question formats, and white mainline Protestants express roughly the same views about evolution regardless of the approach used. Overwhelming majorities of the religiously unaffiliated (those who describe their religion as atheist, agnostic or nothing in particular) say humans have evolved over time on both the two-question (87 percent) and the single-question format (88 percent).

Prior to this recent experiment, the center tested various versions of a two-step approach to asking about evolution. In one line of testing, we varied the survey context (that is, the questions that immediately precede the evolution questions) but found no differences in survey responses. In another line of testing, we varied whether the questions asked about the evolution of "*humans* and other living things" or "*animals* and other living things" and, again, found no differences in opinion about evolution among the U.S. population as a whole.

Considered together, the experiments illustrate the importance of testing multiple ways of asking about evolution. For some people, views about the origins and development of human life are bound up with deeply held religious beliefs. Pew Research Center's goal in designing questions on this topic is to allow respondents to share their thoughts about both the scientific theory of evolution and whether God played a role in the creation and development of life on Earth—and to do so in a way that does not force respondents to choose between science and religion. Indeed, the data show that a sizable share of Americans believe *both* that life on Earth has evolved over time *and* that God played some role in the evolutionary process.

This $100 Million Noah's Ark Theme Park Is a Boring, Homophobic Mess

By Jamie Lee Curtis Taete

> *Kentucky's Ark Encounter theme park was designed to be entertaining to Creationists and non-Creationists alike. I was not entertained.*

IT SEEMS THAT ARK ENCOUNTER, THE $100 million Noah's Ark theme park in Kentucky, isn't doing so great.

According to the Louisville Courier Journal, around 860,000 tickets were sold for the Ark between July 2017 and June 2018, which falls pretty far short of the 2 million in annual ticket sales predicted by Ken Ham, the Ark's creator, before it opened. (A spokesperson for the attraction told the *Courier Journal* that ticket sales did not reflect the number of people who visited due to annual passes and free tickets for under fives. They put the actual number closer to a million.)

Ham has previously blamed multiple factors for the underwhelming performance of the attraction. From local business owners to atheists. But is there a simpler explanation? Is it possible that people don't want to visit the Ark because it sucks?

Before examining this, it's worth looking at what the makers of the Ark were going for when they embarked upon the project. According to Ham, the aim was to produce something so entertaining it would attract Christians and non-Christians alike. "How do you reach the general public in a bigger way?" he asked in an interview last year with the *Washington Post*. "Why not attractions that people will come to the way they go to Disney or Universal or the Smithsonian?" Which, presumably, is why he hired

Patrick Marsh, an attractions designer who has worked on Universal Studios and the Sanrio theme park in Japan, to work on the Ark.

So is the Ark likely to draw in visitors in the same way as Disney or Universal or the Smithsonian? I visited to find out:

Getting to the Ark

Once I'd paid $61.48 (!!!) for my entry ticket and parking, I boarded the shuttle bus that takes you from the parking lot to the Ark, which is located on the other side of some hills.

The Ark—which you first glimpse as the bus crests a hill—is genuinely impressive. As advertised, it is a very, very large replica of Noah's Ark.

IS IT FUN ENOUGH TO CONVERT YOU TO A CREATIONIST BELIEF SYSTEM? Not really. Beyond the initial "wow, that's big" the Ark elicits, it doesn't offer much entertainment value. It's just a large building in a shape you don't typically see large buildings in. It'd be a bit like taking one of those uncontacted Amazonian tribespeople to see an empty Best Buy. They'd almost certainly think the structure was interesting, but I doubt they'd want to have to pay $61.48 to spend a day there.

Entry to the Ark

As you enter the Ark, you go through an extremely optimistic queueing area. Like the kind they have at theme parks that switch back on themselves to cram as many people as possible into a small space. If I had to guess, I would estimate the area could hold a thousand-ish people. When I walked through, there were around ten of us in there.

Then you enter the first section of the Ark. Which, weirdly, is another queueing area, this time themed to look like an animal storage hold. There was room for an extra couple of hundred people. It also did not need that space when I visited.

IS IT FUN ENOUGH TO CONVERT YOU TO A CREATIONIST BELIEF SYSTEM? No. But I guess it doesn't really matter because it seems unlikely anyone will ever actually have to wait in either area.

The Animal Hold

The first proper exhibit on the Ark is a room containing lots of wooden cages with model animals in them.

IS IT FUN ENOUGH TO CONVERT YOU TO A CREATIONIST BELIEF SYSTEM? Not really. The animals aren't interactive and don't move or anything. Maybe if you were some kind of model animal enthusiast it would be cool to see?

The original plan was, apparently, to have live animals in this section. Which would've presumably meant hundreds of distressed, loud, shitting animals crammed into cages in a small space with no natural light. Depending on your tolerance for animal cruelty, that could have been an interesting spectacle, I guess.

The Pre-Flood World

Content-wise, this area has massive potential. It shows what the world was like before the flood, which was apparently lots of people vs. dinosaur gladiator battles, human sacrifices, and people getting eaten by sharks.

But, unfortunately, with the exception of three dioramas, all of that is depicted using a bunch of pictures and text on boards stuck to the wall.

IS IT FUN ENOUGH TO CONVERT YOU TO A CREATIONIST BELIEF SYSTEM? No. I can't imagine it would've taken a massive chunk out of their overall budget to make this section a dark ride or a haunted house or something.

A Bunch of Signs on a Wall

Once you're done reading the signs on the wall of the pre-flood world section, you head on to the next attraction: a bunch of signs on walls. These signs go over things like the shortcomings of evolution and how Noah and his family might have theoretically dealt with things like waste disposal and ventilation. There are also some wax figures of Noah's family.

IS IT FUN ENOUGH TO CONVERT YOU TO A CREATIONIST BELIEF SYSTEM? No. People do not want to read signs on walls. Look at Disney World's Epcot. There's a ride called Test Track, which teaches you about automotive design but is also a roller coaster type thing that goes 65 MPH. It generally has a wait time of about an hour. A couple of hundred feet away, there's a museum-style exhibition hall devoted to explaining technological breakthroughs that's so quiet, you could dump a body in there and it would go unnoticed for days.

The Ark's Living Quarters

Then it's on to the living quarters—a series of rooms showing how Noah and his family might have lived. There's a sign as you enter explaining that they've had to take artistic license while designing the area, because the Bible doesn't give much info on this topic.

They could've used that artistic license to make something cool, like Biblical Wakanda. But instead, they made up a name for Noah's wife (Emzara) and created an exhibit on looms, the single least entertaining object on earth.

IS IT FUN ENOUGH TO CONVERT YOU TO A CREATIONIST BELIEF SYSTEM? No. You can see fake bedrooms and living rooms in an IKEA for free. And you don't have to read a single word about looms while doing it.

Spooky Animal Encounter

This is a couple of dark tunnels that features some taxidermy animals and spooky sound effects.

IS IT FUN ENOUGH TO CONVERT YOU TO A CRE-ATIONIST BELIEF SYSTEM? It's probably the most entertaining thing on the ship, but it doesn't quite manage to be entertaining in the traditional sense. Just when looked at comparative to its surroundings.

Fairy Tale Ark

As you can see in the picture above, the entrance for this area, which is surrounded by giant cutesy animals, looks promising.

But it's a bait and switch. This exhibit is actually designed to teach you that cutesy animals, like the kind of cutesy animals that enticed you into the exhibit, are evil. Because children's books that tell the story of the Ark—i.e. the story of a Neolithic man building a boat large enough to carry two representatives of every species on earth—undermine it by making it seem implausible.

IS IT FUN ENOUGH TO CONVERT YOU TO A CREATIONIST BELIEF SYSTEM? Categorically no. And frankly cruel to all the poor, bored kids that are tricked into entering.

Movies

The Ark has two screening areas that, during my visit, played two movies on loop.

The first, *The Noah Interview*, is set in the time of Noah, and shows him being interviewed about the Ark by a journalist from his local paper. Noah is handsome, level-headed, and nice. The reporter is mean, has a British accent, and says things like, "How long have you been working on this ... *little project*?" while rolling

her eyes. The moody CGI backdrop the interview takes place against looks like a Linkin Park video.

The other film, *As in the Days of Noah*, features the same actors, but is set in the present day, with a staff member from Ark Encounter being interviewed by a reporter from a New York tabloid that runs stories with titles like "Best Sex Change Surgeons on the East Coast" and "Start Walking Ladies! Sharia Law Means Male Drivers Only!" and "Hipsters Aren't Cool Anymore."

IS IT FUN ENOUGH TO CONVERT YOU TO A CREATIONIST BELIEF SYSTEM? The only entertainment here is unintentional, so probably not. Unless you convert ironically.

More Signs

And then it's time for signs again. Room after room after room of signs. More signs than have ever been gathered in one place before. More signs than all the Women's Marches combined. Signs with titles like "Cross-Continent Deposition" and "Paraconformities" and "Polsystrate Fossils" and "The Enigmatic Stonehenge."

IS IT FUN ENOUGH TO CONVERT YOU TO A CREATIONIST BELIEF SYSTEM? No. No no. I challenge you to think of an activity less entertaining than reading a sign about whatever a polsystrate fossil is.

A Christian Graphic Novel

One of the newer additions to the Ark is an exhibit made to look like a graphic novel that tells the story of some college kids questioning their faith (spoiler alert: God turns out to be cool, actually).

IS IT FUN ENOUGH TO CONVERT YOU TO A CREATIONIST BELIEF SYSTEM? Ken Ham described the exhibit as "like walking through the pages of a book." An alternative description would be "like reading a bunch of signs stuck to a wall."

Zoo

Once you're outside the Ark, you can go to a zoo area with zebras and camels and some petting-zoo type animals like donkeys and goats. There are, of course, signs—this time explaining why each animal disproves evolution.

IS IT FUN ENOUGH TO CONVERT YOU TO A CREATIONIST BELIEF SYSTEM? I guess it depends on how you feel about zoos. Seeing animals in captivity makes me kind of sad, so if I'm going to go to one I'd like to see something a bit more exciting than a goat.

Ziplines

Also outside are ziplines that you can ride for an additional charge of $49 to $119. I didn't ride them because ziplines are notoriously unfun. With the exception of zipline instructors and American Gladiators, there is not a person alive who has gone ziplining more than once.

Anti-LGBTQ Bigotry

Anti-LGBTQ bigotry is a big attraction at the theme park, and is smattered generously throughout.

All people who volunteer or work at the park are required to sign a "statement of faith" which explicitly prohibits them from employment if they're gay, bi, or a person who has "attempt[ed] to alter [their] gender by surgery or appearance."

During my visit, I saw multiple ads for something the Ark is hosting called "Sacred: Embracing God's Design for Sexuality" which appears to be some sort of transphobic gay conversion event.

Not satisfied with robbing queer people of employment and their identities, Ken Ham also has an ongoing campaign to "take back the rainbow," which is promoted through a nighttime rainbow light show, and merchandise available in the gift shop.

IS IT FUN ENOUGH TO CONVERT YOU TO A CREATIONIST BELIEF SYSTEM? According to Gallup, the number of people who dislike LGBTQ people is falling each year. To incorporate it so extensively into your attraction seems like probably a bad use of resources.

In Conclusion

IS THE ARK FUN ENOUGH TO CONVERT YOU TO A CREATION-IST BELIEF SYSTEM? No. It is, essentially, a $100 million sign storage unit that costs $50 to visit (plus parking).

Which is kind of a bummer. All kids, even ones dragged to creationist attractions by their parents, deserve to have fun. Just because your parents would rather spend their money on this nonsense than Six Flags or a PS4 game, it doesn't mean you deserve to have a miserable childhood.

It had previously been reported that the makers of the Ark were planning an expansion that would include a Ten Plagues of Egypt thrill ride. But Patrick Kanewske, a spokesperson for the attraction, told me the ride is on ice while they focus on building a new auditorium, a retail and dining area, and a Tower of Babel building which contain "several different exhibits that talk to the Biblical account of the flood."

It sounds unlikely, but hopefully at least one of these will have slightly less signs.

What the Alt-Right Gets Wrong About the Vikings

By Erika Harlitz-Kern

Viking Age Scandinavians were immigrants who traded with the Muslim world and embraced gender fluidity—everything the alt-right despises.

AFTER THE HORRIFIC MASS SHOOTING IN El Paso on Aug. 3, it can no longer be denied that white supremacy is a deadly force in American society. The Unite the Right rally in Charlottesville in August 2017 wasn't a culmination of events but the starting point of a series of acts of racist and extremist violence, which historian Kathleen Belew warns are not isolated incidents but calls for more similar acts.

Belew points out that what unites many of these extreme acts of violence is the publishing of a manifesto before the crime is committed. In these manifestos, the perpetrators explain the reasons for their actions based in a worldview created out of what historian Michael Livingston calls a weaponization of history. Livingston mentions one book in particular that is referenced over and over—namely *Might Is Right or the Survival of the Fittest* published by the pseudonymous Ragnar Redbeard in 1896.

In his book, Redbeard—thought to be a Briton called Arthur Desmond— claims that white Europeans are superior to all other races, women and children are the property of men, and violence is the key to establishing domination. The Scandinavian-sounding pseudonym is not a coincidence: the fetishizing of Vikings is central to the ideology of white supremacy.

But the white supremacists' view of the Vikings is another example of their weaponization of history. In many ways, the Vikings were the antithesis of what the alt-right stands for.

First of all, "viking" is not something you are; it's something you do. It's a job description. The people who are lumped together under the umbrella term "Vikings" were the Danes, the Norse, and the Swedes of late Iron Age Scandinavia who made their living from farming and fishing. A select few of the men went "a-viking," but we don't know the exact reasons for why they went. What we do know is that these men could leave the family farm for extended periods of time without jeopardizing the survival of the family. In other words, the men who went a-viking were expendable.

Viking Age society was patriarchal just like ours, but in contrast to what the alt-right claims, men and women both had status. We know this because people traced their lineage either through their mother or their father, depending on which one had the higher social position. An example of this is the man Alrik who raised a runestone commemorating his father Spjut, who went raiding in the west. On the stone, Alrik introduces himself as the son of Sigrid, his mother. Another example is the runestone commemorating farmer Gulle's five sons, who all died in different parts of the world. The runestone was commissioned by their niece, Torgärd. Runestones were expensive, so for Torgärd to commission a stone she needed to have the agency to act on her own behalf, as well as control over her own personal wealth.

In Viking Age Scandinavian society, certain tasks were strictly gender-coded. To simplify, we say that men did the work outdoors, and women the work indoors. These lines were rarely, if ever, crossed. A Viking Age farm couldn't function without a man-woman couple to run it. This couple could be husband and wife, two siblings, or a parent and a grown child. Which leads to another misconception about the Vikings—that there were only men onboard the longships. The Scandinavian settlements, such as the ones in Newfoundland, Greenland, Iceland, and the British Isles, would never have come into existence without women's participation.

The strict labor division between men and women co-existed with what seems to have been a gender that incorporated both the male and the female. Viking Age burials with female human remains buried with male-coded grave goods point in this direction, as do the myths about shield-maidens.

Evidence of fluid gender boundaries can also be found in Norse mythology. Magic and prophecy were gender-coded female, and the wise woman, or völva, was an important member of the community. But it is Odin who is the god of wisdom, magic, and prophecy. Meanwhile, Loki, the trickster, shape-shifted into a mare and gave birth to Odin's eight-legged horse, Sleipnir.

The resurgence of Norse mythology in the form of Asatrú has attracted followers from the alt-right who follow a racist and misogynist version of it. In the information about Norse religious practices that have survived to our time, there is no support for this sort of interpretation. What's more, the definitive text on Norse mythology is *Snorri's Edda* written and compiled by 13th-century Icelandic historian and lawspeaker Snorri Sturluson. Snorri viewed Norse mythology through the lens of his Christian faith and his knowledge of *The Iliad* and *The Odyssey*. According to *Snorri's Edda*, Odin brought his people out of Asia in search for a new place to live, and this is how the gods—the Æsir—and their home, Asgard, got their names.

Another issue with Asatrú is that it gives the impression that all Viking Age Scandinavians were pagans. When it comes to religion, the Viking Age was a transition period where people were pagans, Christians, or both. Thor hammers made towards the end of the Viking Age could be used as both a hammer and a cross.

In contrast to how the alt-right uses the Vikings for their purposes, Viking Age Scandinavians were raiders turned immigrants who became completely assimilated into their new societies. If it weren't for the introduction of certain Scandinavian dietary practices, place names, and political customs, there is hardly any evidence left of their presence.

Also, they had close contacts with the Muslim world. Viking Age Scandinavia was part of a trade network that reached from the English Channel to the Persian Gulf and which brought goods, people, and impulses to the region from as far away as India. Tens of thousands of Arabic silver coins, minted in today's Iraq, have been found in Sweden alone.

This exchange and interaction brings us to the final point. Viking Age Scandinavians were not tall, blonde, and blue-eyed. The idea of the Viking warrior as the finest specimen of manhood took hold in the late 19th century when racism and Nordicism developed into ideologies declaring Scandinavians to be the superior race. Analyses of human remains from the Viking Age have revealed a wide spectrum of hair color, eye color, and height. Once again, there are echoes in Norse mythology. There, Thor does not look like Chris Hemsworth, but is described as a short and stocky redhead with a full beard and covered in body hair.

Of course, Viking Age Scandinavians were what we today would call white, and they were fierce fighters. But their skin color comes from the fact that they lived in and around the Arctic. And their fighting abilities developed because they lived in a violent society defined by vendettas and power struggles. These things don't make the Vikings superior to anyone else. It makes them typical for the time and place where they lived.

Reading 2.4

Superhero Stories Aren't Myths. They're Anti-Myths.

By Noah Berlatsky

Unlike myths, superhero sagas suggest that justice is actually attainable.

AND LO, LIKE A FIERY PORTENT streaking across the firmament, *Avengers: Infinity War* approacheth! Heroes will triumph, other heroes will die, money will rain down, and marketing will shake the very foundations of the Earth. It will be spectacular, amazing, titanic. It will be *mythic*. Right? Superheroes are often referred to as our "modern mythology." The parallels with and borrowings from Greek or Norse myths are straightforward, and superhero stories generally concern beings with magical strength and amazing abilities who perform incredible feats and have unearthly adventures. Superman rocketed from his home planet Krypton as a baby; that narrative echoes the story of the infant Moses in the bulrushes. The Hulk pounding giant alien invaders in the *Avengers* is like Hercules capturing Cerebus, sort of! The parallels are close enough that many legendary gods have actually been re-tooled as superheroes. Thor and Odin and Loki and Hela from Norse mythology were reimagined in comic book form by Jack Kirby, and now appear regularly in the Marvel Cinematic Universe. Ares, the Greek god of war, showed up to fight Wonder Woman in the 2017 film.

While the similarities between superheroes and myth are real, they're also superficial. Traditional myths in the West concern beings with great powers. Those beings, though, crucially, aren't human; they're gods and demigods and are usually outside of human control. The myths most cited as parallel with superhero stories—Greek myths, Norse myths, Biblical stories—aren't empowerment fantasies. They're stories about terrible forces that control the lives of puny humans, who have no choice but to acquiesce and then die and then, more often than not, go to hell. In contrast, superhero stories tend to be about how, in a godless universe, humans can don super armor, defeat evil, and save everybody while rock music plays. Superhero stories aren't myths. They're anti-myths.

Just about any Greek or Biblical story can illustrate the distinction. Take the myth of Iphigenia. King Agamemnon accidentally violates an arbitrary taboo by killing a deer in a grove that is sacred to the goddess Artemis. In retaliation, Artemis demands that he sacrifice his daughter, or else she will prevent him from sailing to the Trojan War.

In a superhero story, the invulnerable Achilles might go on an adventurous quest to find and defeat the nefarious Artemis (perhaps played by Malin Akerman or some such). But in the story, Iphigenia is generally either whisked away by Artemis at the last moment or, more often, killed. In Euripides' play, in fact, Iphigenia is portrayed as heroic not because she fights injustice, but because she accepts it, and eagerly goes to her death for the glory of Greece.

Bible narratives are also notably skeptical about human agency and empowerment. Jonah isn't bitten by a radioactive orca as a prologue to a thundering battle with the whale. The story of Job isn't about the protagonist self-actualizing by defeating an evil mastermind. It's about God ruining Job's life for no reason, because God can do that.

Like Iphigenia, Job is the plaything of forces beyond his comprehension. In the universe of myth, the existence of super-beings means that humans have *less* power, not more. "Man that is born of a woman is of few days, and full of trouble." That's the subtext—or, in Job's case, the actual text—of the old stories about gods.

Superhero stories completely reverse this idea. It's not an accident that the first superhero lifted his name from Nietzsche's Superman. The whole premise of the superhero is that the Gods are dead and irrelevant, and that humans can, and should, expand to fill the space left in the cosmos by that divine absence.

The typical superhero film is about some flawed guy (it's usually a guy) who lacks self-confidence. But then he gains superpowers, finds his inner strength and humanity, and self-actualizes by saving the innocent and bringing evildoers to justice. Instead of Icarus flying too high and then plummeting to Earth, the superhero flaps those wings and whooshes up to bash that evil sun right in the snoot.

Films like *Guardians of the Galaxy 2* are remarkably explicit in positioning superheroes not as heirs to myths, but as antidotes to them. The film's villain is Ego (Kurt Russell), a godlike being who behaves much like the Greek Gods of myth: He sleeps with lots of women, kills people for obscure reasons, and generally wields his power in an arbitrary and cruel manner because he's a god and can do whatever he wants.

In contrast, his son, Starlord (Chris Pratt), is a typical super-dude who believes that with great power comes great responsibility. Starlord fights his dad on behalf of his friends, innocent bystanders, and general human decency. And, of course, Starlord wins. Get rid of those old myths about human weakness and fate and tragedy. Post-enlightenment, post-Nietzsche, humans have the will, the technology, and the power to set the cosmos to rights.

It's difficult to regret the death of those old myths; no one wants to root for Ego. Destroying lots of planets because you feel like it and you're a jerk is no way to run a multiverse. Superhero stories appeal to our modern sense of justice and morality—which is precisely where they cease to be myths.

In comparison to selfish, philandering, all-powerful jerks like Ego or Zeus, superheroes start to look like a pretty good ethical model, superheroes wouldn't just accept that Iphigenia has to be sacrificed for no reason. Instead they'd feel empowered to confront injustice and evil and to make the world a better place. Give Job a super-suit and let him grab Satan by the horns. If myths say that we should be powerless before injustice, then, yes, let's do away with them and make some anti-myths about getting empowered instead.

Those anti-myths do have some downsides of their own though. Myths once taught us that Gods were mysterious beings beyond our ken. They were often parables about the perils of hubris. Agamemnon was a king, but there were still rules and laws that he had to obey, or else.

The superheroes of anti-myth, though, experience setbacks only to make their ultimate, inevitable victory all the sweeter. The justice of God was insufficient; the justice of Captain America will be better and more satisfying. Superheroes promise: "God is dead—we will save you!" That's a relief. But only if you believe the myth that your fellow humans are kinder and wiser than the gods.

Americans and Their Myths

By Jean-Paul Sartre

OCTOBER 18, 1947

EVERYTHING HAS BEEN SAID ABOUT THE United States. But a person who has once crossed the Atlantic can no longer be satisfied with even the most penetrating books; not that he does not believe what they say, but that his agreement remains abstract.

When a friend tries to explain our character and unravel our motives, when he relates all our acts to principles, prejudices, beliefs, and a conception of the world which he thinks to find in us, we listen uneasily, unable either to deny what he says or entirely accept it. Perhaps the interpretation is true, but what is the truth that is being interpreted? We miss the intimate warmth, the life, the way one is always unpredictable to oneself and also tiresomely familiar, the decision to get along with oneself, the perpetual deliberations and perpetual inventions about what one is, and the vow to be "that" and nothing else—in short, the liberty. Similarly, when a careful arrangement of those melting-pot notions—puritanism, realism, optimism, and so on—which we have been told are the keys to the American character is presented to us in Europe, we experience a certain intellectual satisfaction and think that, in effect, it must be so. But when we walk about New York, on Third Avenue, or Sixth Avenue, or Tenth Avenue, at that evening hour which, for Da Vinci, lends softness to the faces of men, we see the most pathetic visages in the world, uncertain, searching, intent, full of astonished good faith, with appealing eyes, and we know that the most beautiful generalizations are of very little service: they permit us to understand the system but not the people.

The system is a great external apparatus, an implacable machine which one might call the objective spirit of the United States and which over there they call Americanism-a huge complex of myths, values, recipes, slogans, figures, and rites. But one must not think that it has been deposited in the head of each American just as the God of Descartes deposited the first notions in the mind of man; one must not think that it is "refracted" into brains and hearts and at each instant determines affections or thoughts that exactly express it. Actually, it is something outside of the people, something presented to them; the most adroit propaganda does nothing else but present it to them continuously. It is not in them, they are in it; they struggle against it or they accept it, they stifle in it or go beyond it, they submit to it or reinvent it, they give themselves up to it or make furious efforts to escape from it; in any case it remains outside them, transcendent, because they are men and it is a thing.

There are the great myths, the myths of happiness, of progress, of liberty, of triumphant maternity; there is realism and optimism—and then there are the Americans, who, nothing at first, grow up among these colossal statues and find their way as best they can among them. There is this myth of happiness: black-magic slogans warn you to be happy at once; films that "end well" show a life of rosy ease to the exhausted crowds; the language is charged with optimistic and unrestrained expressions—"have a good time," "life is fun," and the like. But there are also these people, who, though conventionally happy, suffer from an obscure malaise to which no name can be given, who are tragic through fear of being so, through that total absence of the tragic in them and around them.

There is this collectivity which prides itself on being the least "historical" in the world, on never complicating its problems with inherited customs and acquired rights, on facing as a virgin a virgin future in which every thing is possible—and there are these blind gropings of bewildered people who seek to lean on a tradition, on a folklore. There are the films that write American history for the masses and, unable to offer them a Kentucky Jeanne d'Arc or a Kansas Charlemagne, exalt them with the history of the jazz singer, Al Jolson, or the composer, Gershwin. Along with the Monroe doctrine, isolationism, scorn for Europe, there is the sentimental attachment of each American for his country of origin, the inferiority complex of the intellectuals before the culture of the old Continent, of the critics who say, "How can you admire our novelists, you who have Flaubert?" of the painters who say, "I shall never be able to paint as long as I stay in the United States"; and there is the obscure, slow effort of an entire nation to seize universal history and assimilate it as its patrimony.

There is the myth of equality—and there is the myth of segregation, with those big beach-front hotels that post signs reading "Jews and dogs not allowed," and those lakes in Connecticut where Jews may not bathe, and that racial *tchin*, in which the lowest degree is assigned to the Slavs, the highest to the Dutch immigrants of 1680. There is the myth of liberty—and the dictatorship of public opinion; the myth of economic liberalism—and the big companies extending over the whole country which, in the final analysis, belong to no one and in which the employees, from top to bottom, are like functionaries in a state industry. There is respect for science and industry, positivism, an insane love of "gadgets"—and there is the somber humor of the New Yorker, which pokes bitter fun at the mechanical civilization of America and the hundred million Americans who satisfy their craving for the marvelous by reading every day in the "comics" the incredible adventures of Superman, or Wonderman, or Mandrake the Magician.

There are the thousand taboos which proscribe love outside of marriage—and there is the litter of used contraceptives in the back yards of coeducational colleges; there are all those men and women who drink before making love in order to transgress in drunkenness and not remember. There are the neat, coquettish houses, the pure-white apartments with radio, armchair, pipe, and stand—little paradises; and there are the tenants of those apartments who, after dinner, leave their chairs, radios, wives, pipes, and children, and go to the bar across the street to get drunk alone.

Perhaps nowhere else will you find such a discrepancy between people and myth, between life and the representation of life. An American said to me at Berne: "The trouble is that we are all eaten by the fear of being less American than our neighbor." I accept this explanation: it shows that Americanism is not merely a myth that clever propaganda stuffs into people's head but something every American continually reinvents in his gropings. It is at one and the same time a great external reality rising up at the entrance to the port of New York across from the Statue of Liberty, and the daily product of anxious liberties. The anguish of the American confronted with Americanism is an ambivalent anguish; as if he were asking, "Am I American enough?" and at the same time, "How can I escape from Americanism?" In America a man's simultaneous answers to these two questions make him what he is, and each man must find his own answers.

Discussion Questions

1. What were the main findings of the Pew Research Center's study of creationism? In what ways did survey respondents navigate the issue of natural evolution versus a God-created universe?
2. In what ways does Ark Encounter market creationist mythology? What are the park's main features, and do you believe it can succeed in the goal of conversion?
3. Reading 2.3 makes the case that Norse and Viking mythology have been appropriated and "weaponized" by the Alt-Right. Do you agree that this is the case? In what ways does the author position historical Vikings as being different than the Alt-Right version?
4. Do you agree with Reading 2.4 that superheroes aren't myths but "anti-myths"? What is the reasoning behind this claim, and how does it stack up against an anthropological definition?
5. Do you agree with Jean-Paul Sartre that "Americanism is not merely a myth that clever propaganda stuffs into people's head but something every American continually reinvents in his gropings?" Why or why not? If so, what do you view to be the features of "Americanism" in the twenty-first century?

Further Readings

Barbour, Ian G. *When Science Meets Religion: Enemies, Strangers, or Partners?* New York: HarperCollins Books, 2000.

> An excellent and accessible study of the relations among theology and religious ideology and scientific perspectives and methods. Barbour places special emphasis on the cosmos, biological evolution, and neurobiology. Throughout, he attempts to address important questions (such as where the universe and humanity come from) from the point of view of how to advance dialogue on all sides of these fraught debates.

Csapo, Eric. *Theories of Mythology*. Hoboken, NJ: Wiley-Blackwell, 2005.

> A comprehensive introduction to various academic perspectives on myth and mythology, drawing on such social science subfields as ritual studies, psychoanalysis, and structuralism.

Dundes, Alan, ed. *Sacred Narrative: Readings in the Theory of Myth*. Berkeley: University of California Press, 1984.

> A collection of analytical essays on world myths edited by one of the world's best-known folklorists.

Eliade, Mircea. *Myth and Reality*. Long Grove, IL: Waveland Press, 1998 [1963].

> This classic investigation of "living" myths by one of the most famous historians of religion looks at how sacred stories give meaning and value to life in a variety of social contexts.

Lévi-Strauss, Claude. *Myth and Meaning: Cracking the Code of Culture*. New York: Schocken, 1995 [1978].

Five lectures originally delivered for radio by the father of structural anthropology. These accessible essays look at the connections among culture, mind, and myth, and summarize interpretations and insights from one of the twentieth century's leading social anthropologists.

Malinowski, Bronislaw. *Myth in Primitive Psychology*. London: Norton [1926].

This classic study by one of the founders of British social anthropology explores the "functional" character or "primitive" myths as stories that explain and situate human life and provide a "road map" for productive social behavior.

Part III

||||||||||||||||||||||||||||||||||||||||||||||||||||||||||||||||||||||||||||||||||||||||||||||||||||||||||||||||||||||||||||||||||||||||||||||||||||

Magical Culture

Introduction

In the United States and around the world, magic evokes the entwined ideas of mystery and largely unseen power. Nevertheless, there is a fair amount of ambiguity surrounding the word as used in everyday speech, mostly because it is so semantically flexible; one can refer to the magic of the atmosphere of Disneyland or the magic of an illusionist showman in Las Vegas; the magic of the Harry Potter novels or the magic of a first kiss. Routinely, we apply the word in a somewhat careless or even sarcastic way to denote things or events that are too difficult or time-consuming to explain systematically or rigorously. (I ask, "How did he get 99 percent on his calculus exam?" You respond, "Magic ... how else?") So, given this eclectic variety of uses, is it even possible or desirable to settle on a fixed definition?

Traditionally, anthropologists have used the term "magic" to refer to the manipulation of transcendent power by a human agent through the use of symbols and generally in the interests of achieving some real-world objective or practical change. This definition is both valuable and inadequate.

It is valuable, first, because it identifies a type of reasoning that can be mapped out in time and space across all human societies. There has never been a human society in which some symbolic thought and activity has not been put toward some practical achievement. This is true whether we are talking about fixing cars, filling cavities, or assuaging spirits whose help we need to "make things right." In each of these examples, magic involves a body of specialized technical knowledge and ability in the hands of an accredited professional who achieves a powerful result, even while the details of his or her action are invisible to untrained eyes. Of course, people will disagree as to whether the activities of neurosurgeons are as symbolic in character as those of traditional shamans and priests, but there is no doubt that medical doctors, too, wield symbolically powerful objects (stethoscopes, lab coats, scalpels, etc.) that together paint a portrait of authority in the minds of the untrained. In this way, this idea that magic and magicians are universal and even archetypal is appealing for comparative analysis of how social institutions function to bestow meaning and order on a largely uncontrollable universe.

On the flip side of this coin (flipping coins, incidentally, is a mundane act of magical divination—fortune-telling—if ever there was one), magic so defined is wholly inadequate for a more perceptive theory of human action, meaning, and motivation. This is because even the idea of magic (let alone the term) is, to use an anthropological phrase, "culture bound." This means that the term carries with it the historical baggage of many hidden assumptions that are difficult to purge in the first place and nearly impossible in the second if we grant the term universal status as a natural fact of human life and culture.

To cite one well-worn example, the logic behind casual usage of the word "magic," as suggested previously, tends to disguise an older, less frivolous application of the term to the religious traditions of non-Europeans, whose rituals seemed exotic, frightening, superstitious, and bizarre. An appropriate modern response to this ethnocentric assertion might be to observe that one person's religion is another person's magic and vice versa. In other words, my beliefs and practices are quite obviously right, logical, and compelling while yours are quite obviously incorrect, illogical, and repulsive. Clearly, religious beliefs and activities that are foreign to our own experience often seem illogical or even frightening. This was perhaps most especially true during the era of European discovery and colonization of the non-Western world (sixteenth to early-twentieth centuries) when most Europeans believed Christianity, science, and Western ways of understanding the world generally were self-evidently superior to the "primitive" practices of Native Americans, Africans, and other indigenous peoples around the globe.

And yet, to a degree that should make us all a bit uncomfortable, such assumptions and the language in which they are embedded (most especially in the words magic and witchcraft) persist into the twenty-first century—albeit in a more innocuous way than at the height of the colonial era. Consider the innocent entertainment value of the Harry Potter and Lord of the Rings sagas by J. K. Rowling and J.R.R. Tolkien, respectively. On the page, both universes are unbridled, sprawling masterpieces of creative ingenuity. Since their commercial popularization as novels, both worlds have found even wider audiences via theatrical films that feature the latest optical effects, bringing to life a host of magical events, characters, and creatures. At least superficially, most of us would agree that such fantasy tales are fiction and, hence, at root unreal—created for the purposes of pure escapism from everyday routines and drudgery. The same might be said of a wide variety of television series grounded in the theme of magical powers and beings. (A mere handful of titles culled from the last few years includes *Charmed*, *Being Human*, *True Blood*, *American Horror Story*, *Fringe*, *Medium*, *Grimm*, *Merlin*, *Heroes*, *Game of Thrones*, *Supernatural*, and the list goes on.) Yet the ways in which such magical universes capture popular attention are not unlike the ways in which earlier generations of Americans were captivated by the mystery and alleged primitiveness of non-Western religious traditions—in particular those connected with Native America and Western Africa. With regard to the latter, the frightening specter of "black magic" and "sorcery" was expressed in a fascination among European and Euro-American whites with Vodou (Haiti) and its sister African Caribbean traditions: Obeah (Jamaica), Santeria (Cuba, Central America), and Candomblé (Brazil). All of these religions are related through common descent from slaves taken from Yoruba, Igbo, Ewe, and Fon peoples. While examination of these traditions has shown them to be complex, subtle, beautiful, and symbolically rich, it continues to be the case that they are regarded by many as both superstitious and primitive, their "magic" derived from a lack of reasoning and knowledge. The distinctions between magic, witchcraft, and sorcery are, in this understanding, blurry to say the least. We should not let the obvious differences between such pop cultural phenomena as the Harry Potter novels and films and Haitian Vodou (aka "Voodoo") obscure what these have in common—that they are attractive in part because they exude a quality of mystery and unknown power that defies conventional rationality. In the case of Rowling's novels, this is unproblematic. But when discussing the authentic religious worlds of living, vibrant societies that have been historically marginalized and culturally dominated (to say the very least), it is hopefully clear how treating such beliefs and rituals as mysterious in contemporary times might hinder rather than help advance an appreciation of these as fully formed and culturally sophisticated religions. It is hard to see how the idea of magic, applied to such historically rich traditions, can be helpful in advancing our knowledge of them.

Returning to the theme of magic in US popular culture, the portrayal of magical culture in media and entertainment—books, film, television series, onstage spectacles, and performance—is, of course, nothing new; it has been happening for many decades. What *is* new is the extent to which the supernatural and natural worlds are increasingly being explained in terms of one another. While the Harry Potter universe has tended to leave to the readers' and viewers' imaginations the question of how magic happens, other popular depictions—among them the *Star Wars* and *Star Trek* sagas—increasingly endeavor to account for what might otherwise be inexplicable powers and events in terms of scientific reality. Consider the way in which the mystical concept of "the Force" in George Lucas's *Star Wars* films underwent a metamorphosis between the original film trilogy (late 1970s and early 1980s) and the second (late 1990s and early 2000s). Rather than leave this transcendent power unexplained, the later films sought to ground it in ideas drawn from genetics, microbiology, and other advanced scientific fields. Lucas put a new spin on the older, vaguely religious idea of an all-powerful and perhaps inscrutable universal essence by invoking fictional microorganisms—"midi-chlorians"—that mediated between the Force and human physiology, bestowing great power on certain individuals. For our discussion, what matters is that Lucas was almost certainly tapping into a blossoming millennial fascination with highly advanced technologies that would seem to hold the promise of uniting theology and science. The appeal of a unified theory of everything is increasingly attractive to a generation disenchanted by the many controversies, scandals, and perceived hypocrisies of traditional religious institutions. Popular sagas like the *Star Wars* films help to articulate this discontent by providing a more satisfactory, if less spiritually demanding, alternative to formal religion that simultaneously generates great excitement and cinematic drama. The lure of the magical—transcendent power available and at work in this world—is almost certainly a key driver of this appeal.

On this note, I cannot complete this introduction without mention of Walt Disney's "magic kingdom." In the nineteenth century, French sociologist Émile Durkheim famously discussed the power of social ritual to generate a transcendent emotional and physiological experience of what he called "collective effervescence." Perhaps no better single instance of this experience in US culture can be found than the vast, multiplatform, and impressively lucrative world of Disney films, theme parks, television, music, and toys. If we expand Durkheim's idea to incorporate the ritualization of everyday childhood activities, centered on viewing movies and television, listening to and singing songs, playing video games, playing with toys, and dressing up in glittering, character-themed costumes, it is clear that the effervescent emotion he referred to is real for children—many millions of whom experience this imagined world across multiple domains. But even if we consider solely the in-person social community that forms at Disney theme parks (closer to what Durkheim had in mind), it is clear what the term "magic" is intended to convey when applied to this context. Recent visits to Disneyland with my daughter and several of her young schoolmates leave little doubt in my mind as to the impact of this place on a child's imagination. Developmentally, children are emotionally and physiologically receptive to new vistas of spectacle, sound, and color; the thrill that comes from encountering beloved storybook characters; eating normally verboten foods in abundance (cotton candy, soda, and massive ice-cream cones for dinner, anyone?); and experiencing out-of-the-ordinary events in an out-of-the-ordinary way (riding thrilling roller coasters at nighttime and watching colorful parades well into the evening come to mind). What is this powerful, transformative experience if *not* magic? The term is appropriate in relation both to the storybook fairy tales of the Disney universe and the impact of these in the context of overwhelming theme park experiences. Acquisition by Disney Studios of parallel magical universes in the form of Pixar films and characters, Marvel Comics heroes, and all the vast world of *Star Wars* seems poised to generate new synergies of transcendent experience, particularly for children (and, as the expression goes, "children at heart").

While many have wondered whether religion is being eroded by a nonreligious or secular society, one might just as easily ask whether it is really the character of public interest in the transcendent that has changed (together with its rituals, heroes, and institutions) rather than its fundamental appeal. While it cannot be denied that there is an ongoing tension in US society between commitment to traditional forms of religion and newer, media-driven, "nonreligious" religions like *Star Wars*, Harry Potter, *Star Trek*, and the Disney universe, neither can the emotional and socially compelling character of these forms of secular (yet transcendently oriented) "magic" be ignored. The readings in this part focus on a wide range of "magical" experiences, encounters, and even marketing strategies that reveal much about contemporary American perspectives on the transcendent universe. Some of these, such as the very traditional Catholic phenomenon of weeping statues and the widespread Pentecostal practice of "speaking in tongues," assume that unseen power and agency are active in the human world to bring messages of different kinds. Others, such as those describing the ritualization and marketing of beauty practices and the "magical consciousness" of the fashion industry suggest both a deep desire for and hope that transcendent power is subject to manipulation for individual benefit. Still, another looks to neurological research to uncover the hidden evolutionary biology of magical reasoning. In sum, these readings help us to understand how magic is all around us—even if it's not.

Believers Flock to Virgin Mary Statue "Crying" Red Tears

By Rich Pedroncelli

SACRAMENTO (AP)—CARRYING ROSARY BEADS AND cameras, the faithful have been coming in a steady stream to a church on the outskirts of Sacramento for a glimpse of what some are calling a miracle: A statue of the Virgin Mary they say has begun crying a substance that looks like blood.

It was first noticed more than a week ago, when a priest at the Vietnamese Catholic Martyrs Church spotted a stain on the statue's face and wiped it away. Before Mass on Nov. 20, people again noticed a reddish substance near the eyes of the white concrete statue outside the small church, said Ky Truong, 56, a parishioner.

According to a deacon at Vietnamese Catholic Martyrs Church, the red "tears" on this statue came back after being wiped away at first.

Since then, Truong said he has been at the church day and night, so emotional he can't even work. He believes the tears are a sign.

"There's a big event in the future—earthquake, flood, a disease," Truong said. "We're very sad."

On Saturday, tables in front of the fenced-in statue were jammed with potted plants, bouquets of roses and candles. Some people prayed silently, while others sang hymns and hugged their children. An elderly woman in a wheelchair wept near the front of the crowd.

A red trail could be seen from the side of the statue's left eye to about halfway down the robe of concrete.

"I think that it's incredible. It's a miracle. Why is she doing it? Is it something bothering her?" asked Maria Vasquez, 35, who drove with her parents and three children from Stockton, about 50 miles south of Sacramento.

Thousands of such incidents are reported around the world each year, though many turn out to be hoaxes or natural phenomena.

The Diocese of Sacramento has so far not commented on the statue, and the two priests affiliated with the church did not return a telephone message Saturday.

The Rev. James Murphy, deacon of the diocese's mother church, the Cathedral of the Blessed Sacrament, said church leaders are always skeptical at first.

"For people individually seeing things through the eyes of faith, something like this can be meaningful. As for whether it is supernatural or a miracle, normally these incidences are not. Miracles are possible, of course," Murphy said. "The bishop is just waiting and seeing what happens. They will be moving very slowly."

But seeing the statue in person left no doubt for Martin Operario, 60, who drove about 100 miles from Hayward. He took photos to show to family and friends.

"I don't know how to express what I'm feeling," Operario said. "Since religion is the mother of believing, then I believe."

Nuns Anna Bui and Rosa Hoang, members of the Salesian Sisters of San Francisco, also made the trek Saturday. Whether the weeping statue is declared a miracle or not, they said, it is already doing good by awakening people to the faith and reminding them to pray.

"It's a call for us to change ourselves, to love one another," Hoang said.

Why Magic-Inspired Routines Are a Growing Beauty Trend

By Hannah Betts

T HE LANGUAGE OF BEAUTY IS AWASH with magic. 'Let me be spellbinding,' yearns the teenager in all of us; the word 'glamour' derives from an early-18th-century term meaning 'enchantment'. Fairy-tale transformations remain perennially thrilling, from the old-woman-turned-beauty of Chaucer's *The Wife of Bath's Tale* to the ravishing sorceress Melisandre in *Game of Thrones*, whose pulchritude relies upon a flaming jewel. Since the solstice drew near—when the days became long and the nights rich in promise—who didn't pondered her own occult ritual, à la Cassandra Mortmain in *I Capture the Castle*, to conjure beauty, charm and the love that feels attendant on both?

Well, we're in luck because the beauty industry is becoming one big mystical love-in, the word 'magic' supplanting 'natural' as the obsession du jour.

Charlotte Tilbury has her Magic Cream, Anastasia of Beverly Hills her Moonchild Glow Kit, Lush its bathing wares based on mediaeval potions.

Crystal-infused beauty is everywhere from cleanser (Aveda's Botanical Kinetics Exfoliating Crème Cleanser) to highlighter (Glossier's Haloscope in Topaz), while big business is becoming ever more open-minded in its embrace of more arcane wares: with Estée Lauder Companies now selling chakra sprays and Selfridges stocking Psychic Sisters' Bath Salts and Candles.

In an age in which reality feels at once too real and surreal, while technology drains our psyches, it makes sense that many of us are looking beyond the mundane.

As a dogmatic atheist, I tend to find my bewitchment in material miracles: Dr Michael Prager's sorcery with a Botox needle, say, or Bobbi Brown's miraculous foundations. Nevertheless, even I feel the draw of higher mysteries.

Ila Spa's founder, Denise Leicester, describes herself as a nurse, aromatherapist, yoga teacher, sound healer, holistic bodyworker and spiritual philosopher. Her brand has been created with 'conscious, healing intent', and fans of her philosophy of beauty as 'soul sustenance' include Gwyneth Paltrow, Natalie Portman and Donna Karan.

I visit the Lanesborough Spa to experience one of Ila's crystal-singing-bowl therapies, which offers an 'internal massage' through vibration with the chakras. After a mere 20 minutes, I emerge becalmed and—yes!—more fetching, my face having lost its customary tense rictus.

My beloved frequently inquires why there's a chunk of pink rock by our bed, to which I respond: 'It's why we are together!' rose quartz supposedly being a purveyor of love. In truth, I simply love the look of crystals: earthen jewels with the childish appeal of collecting pebbles on the beach. However, those who argue in favour of crystals' spiritual properties claim that they transmit stable energy to anchor vacillating human emotions. Enthusiasts include Adele, Victoria Beckham, Lena Dunham, Cara Delevingne, Miranda Kerr and the Olsen twins; the Duchess of Sussex's black onyx pendant is understood to be a conduit for peace, love and harmony.

"Crystals and their apparent healing properties have become hugely popular," agrees Newby Hands, the global beauty director at Net-A-Porter. "Today's women are very connected to the idea that health, happiness and a glowing skin are directly related, meaning anything that gives us an antidote to stress, lack of sleep, or always feeling we have to be 'on' sells incredibly well."

"We have Kora's Rose Quartz Heart Facial Sculptor, and Angela Caglia's rose quartz Face Rollers, as well as Gua Sha tools, which boost the lymphatic system", Hands continues. "Hi-tech LED-light-therapy masks are a big seller, but we are seeing the same woman buying a jade or crystal roller."

The make-up artist Laurey Simmons is the author of *The Inner Beauty Bible*, which offers a pick 'n' mix of sacred options, beauty rituals included. Accordingly, I bathe my crystals in moonlight, smudge away negative energy using sacred wood, sprinkle petals in my bath and burn precious oils. I embrace the imperfections that come with my 48 years by contemplating a withered leaf, while chanting: 'In beauty may I walk'.

Alas, sacred wood apart (it smells sublime), I feel both irritated and foolish. Still, my distaste for spiritual platitudes propels me towards my own secular strategies, in which applying my morning make-up, brushing my hair, or dousing myself in scent can become moments of heightened awareness. A soak in the bath doesn't have to be otherworldly to anchor me in the beauty of the moment.

Reading 3.3

Why We Talk in Tongues

By T. M. Luhrmann

L AST MONTH I WAS IN ACCRA, Ghana, to learn more about the African version of the new charismatic Christian churches that have become so popular in the United States and are now proliferating in sub-Saharan Africa, especially Ghana and Nigeria. What struck me was how much people spoke in tongues: language-like sounds (usually, repeated phonemes from the speaker's own language) thought by those who use them to be a language God knows but the speaker does not.

I went to services that lasted three hours and for most of which people prayed in tongues. People I interviewed spoke about praying by themselves in tongues for similar stretches of time. They said they did so because it was the one language the devil could not understand, but what I found so striking was how happy it seemed to make them. "We love to speak in tongues," one young Ghanaian woman told me with a laugh.

Some of the early Christians spoke in tongues. At least, the Apostle Paul writes about them in his first letter to the Corinthians. Then, for the most part, tongues died out of Christian practice until Pentecostalism emerged around the turn of the 20th century, most famously at a revival in Los Angeles in 1906. "Weird babel of tongues, new sect of fanatics is breaking loose, wild scene last night on Azusa Street, gurgle of wordless talk by a sister," one newspaper article screamed.

Most tongue speakers talk about tongues as a "gift" from God that can neither be forced nor controlled. Yet the act involves learning and skill. It can also be easily faked. (If you say "I should have bought a Hyundai" 10 times fast, you'll have done just that, a pastor taught me.)

At an American charismatic evangelical church I studied, about a third of the congregants spoke in tongues occasionally when praying alone. As one young man put it: "You run out of things to pray for and you just need to pray, to let all these emotions run out of your head. So you pray in tongues. I do that quite often." The Pew Research Center found that 18 percent of Americans spoke in tongues at least several times a year.

What dawned on me in Accra is that speaking in tongues might actually be a more effective way to pray than speaking in ordinary language—if by prayer one means the mental technique of detaching from the everyday world, and from everyday thought, to experience God.

There are, broadly speaking, two kinds of Christian prayer practice, beyond rote recitation. "Apophatic" prayer, which looks a lot like meditation and mindfulness, asks one to still the mind and disengage from thought. The classic example is the 14th century "Cloud of Unknowing," a monastic text whose anonymous author advised: "Thought cannot comprehend God. And so, I prefer to abandon all I can know, choosing rather to love him who I cannot know."

In "kataphatic" prayer, one fills one's imagination with thoughts from Scripture. The classic example is the 16th-century spiritual exercises of St. Ignatius of Loyola, who called worshipers to see "with the eye of the imagination the road from Nazareth to Bethlehem, considering how long it is and how wide, and whether it is level or goes through valleys and over hills." American evangelicals seeking daydreamlike encounters with God are praying in this tradition.

The apophatic method is probably more effective in shifting attention from the everyday, but harder to achieve. That seems to be what the fifth-century monk Pseudo-Dionysius the Areopagite meant when he described kataphatic prayer as a steppingstone for those who could not pray in other ways. Many of us know people who have tried to meditate and failed, defeated by thoughts that refused to stay put—what skilled practitioners call "monkey mind." In an experiment, I assigned participants for one month to meditation, to imagination-rich prayer or to lectures on the gospels. Many who meditated didn't like it; those who did reported deep spiritual experiences, like the expert meditators studied by the neurologist James H. Austin ("Zen and the Brain") and other scientists.

As a technique, tongues capture the attention but focus it on something meaningless (but understood by the speaker to be divine). So it is like meditation—but without the monkey mind. And the practice changes people. They report that as their prayer continues, they feel increasingly more involved. They feel lighter, freer and better. The scientific data suggest that tongue speakers enter a different mental state. The neuroscientist Andrew B. Newberg and his colleagues took M.R.I. scans of tongue speakers singing worship songs, and then speaking in tongues. When they did the latter, they experienced less blood flow to the frontal cerebral cortex. That is, their brain behaved as if they were less in a normal decision-making state—consistent with the claim that praying in tongues is not under conscious control.

Speaking in tongues still carries a stigmatizing whiff. In his book "Thinking in Tongues," the philosopher James K. A. Smith describes the "strange brew of academic alarm and snobbery" that flickered across a colleague's face when he admitted to being a Pentecostal (and, therefore, praying in tongues). It seems time to move on from such prejudice.

Why Babies (and Perhaps All of Us) Care About Magic

By Susana Martinez-Conde

W E BASE OUR EVERYDAY BEHAVIOR ON thousands of predictions about how reality will unfold around us as we interact with our physical and social environment. Some of our expectations are the product of hard-won experience and direct interaction with the world. Other expectations are programmed in infancy, and hard-wired into our neural systems with little or no exposure to external stimulation. Scientists refer to the latter set of expectations as "core knowledge". Some examples of it are our understanding that solids will not go through walls, or that objects will fall if dropped.

Magic acts hinge on defying all sorts of expectations about the way things should be. Confronted with the violation of their core predictions, audiences become captivated. The most jaded spectator can feel a kind of childlike wonder in front of a talented magician. A new research study investigating how babies react to violations of their prior expectations may explain why magic is so compelling to audiences of all ages.

Aimee E. Stahl and Lisa Feigenson from Johns Hopkins University thought that violations of one's expectations about the world might signal special opportunities for learning. Previous research had shown that babies stare for longer times when their expectations are violated; for instance, if a ball appears to pass through a wall rather than being stopped by the wall, or when an actor approaches someone mean rather than someone nice. It was not known however, whether the babies' increased interest in entities that didn't behave as they should had any cognitive utility.

The scientists hypothesized that violations of expectations might provide opportunities to learn about the world. If so, infants should preferentially learn new information about objects that violate expectations, seek information about those objects, and explore the objects in such a way as to test possible explanations for their bizarre behavior.

The researchers tested one hundred and ten 11-month old infants in an elegant series of experiments. First, the babies watched as toy cars or balls went through walls or were stopped by them (among other physically possible and impossible scenarios). Then, the scientists showed the babies something new about the object they had just observed: for instance, that it squeaked when pushed. The babies learned to associate the sound with the object only if the object had violated their expectations previously. This meant that learning was not generally enhanced following a violation-scenario, but was restricted to the specific objects that violated the babies' expectations.

Next, the scientists had the babies watch events that were either congruent with, or in violation of, basic principles such as object solidity (the object appeared to pass through walls) and object support (the object appeared to hover unsupported in midair). Then, the infants had the opportunity to explore and play with the object they had just watched (the target object) and also with a new object (distractor object). The babies spent more time exploring the target object if it had previously violated core principles. When the object behaved consistently with their expectations, babies played equally with the target and distractor objects. Even more fascinating, the children interacted with target objects that had violated expectations in ways that critically depended on the type of violation observed. The babies who had seen the object go through a wall banged it repeatedly against the table, as if testing its consistency, whereas the babies that had seen the object float in the air dropped it over and over again. That is, the kids tailored their explorations to the type of violation witnessed. This dissociation indicates that the babies were not just reacting in random ways to the surprising scenarios, but were systematically testing their environments, much as scientists do when puzzled by an unpredicted piece of data.

The study concluded that violations of expectations, whether learned or innate, provide special learning opportunities in babyhood and early childhood.

But what about adults confronting the unexpected?

As adults, we don't often experience radical violations of our expectations, particularly those that concern core principles of object behavior. One important exception is magic—A magic performance turns our reasonable expectations upside down: objects vanish, levitate and metamorphose. What if each of these violations signals a unique learning opportunity not only to the infant brain but to the adult brain as well? It may be that magic performances are so compelling because we are wired to engage our minds and actions in unexpected situations.

At the Magic of Consciousness Symposium that Stephen Macknik and I co-hosted in 2007 in Las Vegas, Teller, the mute half of the magician duo Penn and Teller, eloquently proposed that much of our lives is devoted to understanding cause and effect, and that magic "provides a playground for those rational skills". A baby's playground is as large as the world, filled with everyday wonder and opportunity. As we age and learn, the amazement and playfulness shrinks—but we can always rely on magic for a visitor's pass to the stunning playground of the mind.

Magical System

By Brian Moeran

Suit Yourself

"First Look at Spring," "Fashion's Hottest Summer Shade," "Autumn's Key Look," and "Your Style This Winter": fashion magazine headlines take you effortlessly through nature's and the fashion industry's seasons, with their "best buys," "new looks," and "must haves." They ensorcel you with "adventurous" lingerie in "sleek" satin, "breezy" blouses with "ruffled" folds, "care-worn" jeans in "funky" denim, "dazzling" dresses with "dramatic" sleeves, "girlish" skirts with "strategic" zips, "graceful" gowns with "flamboyant" gatherings, "intricate" bodices in "crumpled" cotton, "luxurious" coats in "rich" velvets, "racy" shorts in "sexy" suede, "sassy" suits with "bold" collars, "slinky" jerseys in "skimpy" silk, and a "tailored tux." To these are added "over-the-top" or "low-key" accessories that are so "alluring": "angelic" earrings, "bondage-esque" bracelets, "cute" clutches, "delicate" boas, "elegant" scarves, "feminine" trinkets, "floppy" or "graphic pussy-cat" bows, "jaunty" caps, "jazzy" ankle socks, "no-nonsense" belts, "prim" boots, "saucy" stilettos, "seductive" shoes, "sparkly" sequins, "statement" bags, "strappy" sandals, and a "witty" choker: all leading to "856 pages of spectacular fall fashion!"

The world of fashion is pervaded by a *magical consciousness*, which comes across in all kinds of different situations and contexts, and informs and shapes both individual behaviour and the organization of the fashion world. We can find it among designers, photographers, fashion magazine editors, stylists, makeup artists, models, and so on, as well as among brand-name fashion houses and their seasonal collections. It permeates fashion itself, as clothes are seen to provide occasions for enchantment, illusion, glamour, and charm, allowing transformations of bodily awareness typical of magical transformations found in societies usually studied by anthropologists: "the look is modern in an old-fashioned kind of way"; "Cutting glamorous evening fabrics into simple daywear shapes"; and "When did coloured lingerie become chic rather than tarty?"

Fashion magazines also cast numerological spells: "5 Spring Must-Haves," "12 Perfect Summer Looks," "36 Styles You'll Love," "49 Wanna-Buy-Now Swimsuits," "50 Best Autumn Shoes and Handbags," "52 Page Dictionary of

Paris Brands," "88 Summer Items," "96 Mid-Winter Fashion Finds," "101 Bargains," "105 Casual Looks You'll Wear Anywhere," "120 Pages of Hot Trends," "138 Figure-Fixers," "275 Objects of Desire," "394 Smart Ways to Look Sexy," and "498 Best Buys." You may be able to count on anything in order to be in fashion, but somewhere, surely, there's "a fine line between looking glamorous and looking like a Womble." So where do you draw that line if "the essence of fashion lies in a process of change" (Blumer 1969, 278)? If "fashion" means to "be in fashion" (Blumer 1969, 280), then all you can do is suit yourself and hope for the best.

Each fashion season presents women who read fashion magazines with a cyclical dilemma. Or, rather, fashion magazines first conjure up the dilemma that they then attri-

FIGURE 3.5.1 "The look is modern in an old-fashioned kind of way" (Carolyn Murphy by David Slijper, for *Harper's Bazaar* UK, December 2014).

bute to the season. What should women wear that will carry them seamlessly from day to night ("Make the New Looks Work for You"), dressing up or dressing down according to time, place, and occasion, as the weather warms up or cools down: "Suit of the Season: Seven Days, Seven Ways"; "Workwear Now"; "Evening Essentials"; and "It's Time to Party." How to make that effortless transition from "cool and classic" to "colorful city chic," as you "update your wardrobe," "accentuate your assets," and "maximize your look." Fashion magazines reassure you that you can "cherry pick a personal style, picking up on an idea here and an item there, rather than buying into a look wholesale," but they also consecrate by advising you in formulaic style what the 10 "key looks" of spring or autumn are, as well as "what's in, what's out," to help you toe the seasonal line. Hello "tailored pantsuit," "conical heel pump," and "blouson dress." Goodbye "loose cropped suit," "platform pump," and "shift dress."

And if you wonder at the speed with which you exchange such greetings with your clothes, there's always a helpful hint to cope with the seeming arbitrariness of such change ("making the most of what you've got"). Fashion magazines insist that each item has its purpose: they allude to the virtues of clothing that are transmitted through contact ("a delicate lace trim gives Chanel's white vest subtle sex appeal"), thereby suggesting that sympathetic magic is inherent in fashion ("create a vertical illusion with pinstripes") (see Mauss 1972, 58). The blouson dress "hides hips and flattens the tummy"; the pantsuit jacket "disguises a full bust and gives the appearance of a slim figure," while the slit ankles on pants "hide the bust by drawing the eyes to shapely legs."[1] The airs that you don this season should come on "a platform not a cone."

Performing Magic

> I guess you could say that a fashion story's rather like a piece of music. It should have its own special rhythmical beat. And what you need in order to get that beat is intuition. You have to create a thread to each page. The difficulty is how best to put across that page's contents, rather than just make it look good. For that you need hard work and an occasional bit of magic.[1]

Both the staging of fashion shows and the portrayal of fashions in the fashion magazines involve the performance of magic ("Galliano weaves magic at Haute Couture collections"; "Ten magical moments from Fashion Week"). The time and place of each are prescribed, as the magicians—designers, on the one hand, editors, stylists, photographers, models and art directors, on the other—effect *transformations* ("Nicola Formichetti ... works his transformational magic"). This is why the magical rites of catwalk shows and magazine fashion pages tend not to be performed just anywhere, but in specially qualified places (such as an unused warehouse, studio, or exotic location) (Mauss 1972, 46), which allow them to be effective, to *do* things, and so to "consecrate" (Mauss 1972, 19, 47). Consider, in this light, Alexander McQueen's use of a "breathtakingly beautiful phantom-like" hologram of Kate Moss at his "Widows of Culloden" collection (Fall/Winter 2006–2007):

> As the figure dissolved back into the wisp of light and then faded into the darkness, it seemed as if some magical force had materialized over the runway and then slipped out of sight. Like an apparition—bewildering yet beguiling—it had held the audience spellbound. (Mankoff 2014, 110)

Here magic is intimately entwined with technological sophistication. This leads to the inevitable conclusion that "magic encompasses any activity that society *construes* as being essential to the success of a technique, but that has no *objective* function in the physical mechanics of the process itself" (Suchman 1989, 1272, 1277).

The fashion system endows some designers with charismatic authority, the legitimacy of which rests on "the belief in magical powers, revelations, and hero worship," as well as on the fact that "designers personify the clothes they design" (Kawamura 2005, 62, 65). As a result, it is often a designer's "star quality" that takes precedence over any skills that s/he possesses (Kawamura 2005, 64).

A fashion show is in many ways like the kind of performance put on by healers among the Gnau in New Guinea. For a start, both are preceded by endless preparations, all of which are secret and hidden. Those taking part in the treatment for an illness caused by the spirit Panu'et, for example, follow closely contemporary designers' attention to makeup, hairstyling, and accessories: "First, they must paint its face, prepare its head-dress, and decorate it with shells, feathers and ornaments; then by spells and spitting, they make the spirit go into the image" (Lewis 1986, 424). Designers may not spit, but they do explain how their collections are imbued with some kind of spirit or *zeitgeist* (Vangkilde 2013, 82). This is supposed to emerge in the performance, which is public, and quite short (ideally 12 minutes in the case of each; Carolina Herrera in Koblin 2014, E1, E15; Lewis 1986, 424).

Fashion shows share similarities, too, with séances put on by Siberian shamans:

> When a shaman goes into action the result is not a rite but a séance, which is full of drama and which the people enjoy immensely. A typical performance is a summoning of spirits, and is carried out in the dark … in a house, a tent, or an Eskimo igloo. The people all gather, and the shaman says what he is going to do, after which he puts out the lamps and the re, being sure that there is little or no light. Then he begins to sing … (Howells 1985, 104).

The parallels here with the fashion show are obvious, right down to lighting and music. Moreover, the crescendo of noise that summons the spirits at the start of the séance is akin to the summoning of the fashion models onto the runway (the sole area that is lit). The fashion show, like the séance, involves "a combination of expert showmanship and management" (Howells 1985, 104). In a way, too, it suggests a kind of "autohypnosis, so that while the shaman knows perfectly well he is faking much of the performance he may at the same time work himself into a trance in which he does things he believes are beyond his merely human powers" (Howells 1985, 104). Is the designer, then, a kind of shaman?

Note

1. Personal interview, Takeshi Kawamura, creative director, *Vogue Nippon*, 21 September 2004.

References

Blumer, Herbert. 1969. "Fashion: From Class Differentiation to Collective Selection." *The Sociological Quarterly* 10 (3): 275–291.

Howells, William. 1985. "The Shaman: A Siberian Spiritualist." In *Magic, Witchcraft, and Religion: An Anthropological Study of the Supernatural* (5th edition), edited by

Arthur C. Lehmann and James L. Myers, pp. 91–98. Mountain View, CA: Mayfield Publishing Company.

Kawamura, Yuniya. 2005. *Fashion-ology: An Introduction to Fashion Studies*. Oxford, UK: Berg.

Lewis, Gilbert. 1986. "The Look of Magic." *Man* (N.S.) 21 (3): 414–437.

Mankoff, Debra. 2014. *The Fashion Muse*. Munich, Germany: Prestel.

Mauss, Marcel. 1972. *A General Theory of Magic*. London: Routledge & Kegan Paul.

Suchman, Mark C. 1989. "Invention and Ritual: Notes on the Interrelation of Magic and Intellectual Property in Preliterate Societies." *Columbia Law Review* 89 (6): 1264–1294.

Vangkilde, Kasper. 2013. "In Search of a Creative Concept in HUGO BOSS." In *Exploring Creativity: Evaluative Practices in Innovation, Design, and the Arts*, edited by B. Moeran and B. T. Christensen, pp. 69–95. Cambridge, UK: Cambridge University Press.

Discussion Questions

1. Describe the phenomenon of the "weeping statue." Why do you think such objects are appealing, and how do church officials feel about them? Would you consider this phenomenon to be "magical"?
2. In what ways are magical and "miraculous" therapies and holistic techniques being used in the modern beauty and fashion industries? Do you believe these to be socially healthy (or beneficial) aspects of consumer culture? What do these institutions say about broader American notions of what a perfect society and perfect people would look like?
3. What does it mean to "speak in tongues," and how might one interpret this as a magical activity? In a different way, how might tongues be framed as a distinctive psycho-cognitive discipline?
4. What is "core knowledge," and what does its presence or absence mean for beliefs about magic? What about infancy, in particular, is important for understanding the experience of magic?
5. In what ways do you think traditional religious education and observance promote magical thinking in children? Is this detrimental to their socialization as rational adults and their ability to distinguish fantasy from reality? Even if this is the case, does it matter? Why? Why not?

Further Readings

Copenhaver, Brian P. *Magic in Western Culture: From Antiquity to Enlightenment*. Cambridge: Cambridge University Press, 2015.

A comprehensive survey of magic practice and belief from the ancient Mediterranean and Near East through medieval and early modern Europe. Copenhaver treats magic as a coherent intellectual and philosophical tradition rather than a marginal aspect of religious studies.

Hill, Annette. *Paranormal Media: Audiences, Spirits and Magic in Popular Culture*. Abingdon, UK: Routledge, 2010.

An introduction to the recent mainstreaming of ideas about the transcendent and paranormal in contemporary Anglo-US culture, Hill explores changes in how people have sought to have direct experience of spirits and magical power from the nineteenth through twenty-first centuries. Such encounters range from relatively direct participation through ghost hunting and use of psychic mediums, to sustained interest in transcendent-themed television shows and theatrical films.

Nickell, Joe. *Looking for a Miracle: Weeping Icons, Relics, Stigmata, Visions, and Healing Cures*. Amherst, NY: Prometheus Books, 1999.

In this accessible work written for a nonspecialist readership, popular historian Nickell examines the scientific and cultural bases for a large range of examples drawn from the world of magical faith healing. Specifically, he seeks to examine the hard evidence behind claims concerning visions, weeping statues, and other miracles. In so doing, he hopes to understand whether credulous people have been duped or whether they have insight that transcends the pronouncements of science.

Luhrmann, T. M. *When God Talks Back: Understanding the American Evangelical Relationship with God.* New York: Vintage Books, 2012.

Based on the anthropological research of US evangelicals, this is an important and accessible study of the connections between the act of prayer and psychological and cognitive experience.

Jones, Graham M. *Magic's Reason: An Anthropology of Analogy.* Chicago: University of Chicago Press, 2017.

A historically rich exploration of the interrelations between anthropological study of the colonial world and the practices of entertainment-oriented magic and illusion-ism—particularly insofar as both reveal a deep ambivalence and complex relationship with modernity and Enlightenment rationality.

Part IV

||||||||||||||||||||||||||||||||||||||||||||||||||||||||||||||||||||||||||||||||||||||||||||||||||||||||||||||||||||||||||||||||||||||||||||||||||||||||||||||||||||||

The Living Dead Among Us

Introduction

Among the most popular supernatural beings to instill dread and (paradoxically) longing into the imaginations of modern Westerners are those creatures belonging to the folkloric category of *revenant* (a term adapted from a French verb that means "to return"). While many mysterious and dangerous beings of different times and places are covered by this umbrella term (from the Philippine Asuang to the English will-o'-the-wisp), in the contemporary United States, we have a particular fixation on the concepts of the zombie, the vampire, and the ghost. Arguably, in the modern United States, such beings, entities, or creatures receive far more attention and popular acclaim than gods and other higher-level "powers." While this would, of course, seem blasphemous to some, it is clear from the abundance of novels, television series, feature films, video games, and other media that there is an abiding fascination in "other-than-human" persons, to employ anthropologist Irving Hallowell's phrase. In the Western religious traditions (and beyond), angels and saints often stir up similar fascination and devotion. Still, it is mostly to the darker and morally ambiguous creatures, and not to the fixtures of religious tradition, that popular US culture turns when seeking excitement and the thrill of otherworldliness.

The creature we call the zombie has enjoyed a long history within horror films, comic books, and other pulp fiction. At the time of this writing, zombies are enjoying something of a renaissance on the small screen in AMC's critically acclaimed series *The Walking Dead*. Other big-budget incarnations have included 2004's *Dawn of the Dead* and the popular *28 Days/Weeks After* and

Resident Evil series. In the imagination of popular culture, zombies terrify for their "inhuman" natures. Once human, they are now either dead flesh or diseased beyond repair. Perhaps the most terrifying of their traits is their insatiable hunger for living human flesh. In these ways, the cinematic zombie embodies some of the deepest terrors possible for human beings: a complete loss of life and humanity symbolized by cannibalism (after all, the terror, though real, would doubtless be less jarring if these creatures were feral cats and not human beings). While a full discussion of the origins of the zombie concept is beyond the scope of this introduction, the Haitian zombie—a shambling, soulless figure to be pitied more than feared—provides a clue as to just how far Western culture has departed from original ideas concerning the living dead. In the Haitian countryside, where zombification has served historically as a form of capital punishment for antisocial behavior, the deepest fear imaginable is not *of* zombies but of *becoming* a zombie. In Western culture, this nuance has been upended: being dead-yet-alive has its own terrors that have little to do with depriving individuals of an afterlife. The popular American zombie embodies not just the deepest fears of the animalistic in humanity but also reflects ideas about an apocalyptic end to human society—invariably, zombie stories invoke ideas about great punishment against all humans for our sins. In this sense, they reflect a sobering moral caution of the Judeo-Christian tradition.

Vampires play something of a different role in the popular imagination, and, consequently, their stature in the media of film, television, and books is different from that of the zombie. In 1897, Bram Stoker's seminal fictional creation, Count Dracula, certainly embodied late Victorian ideas about the dangerous, primitive, and wild reaches of southeastern Europe and was a true portrait of terror (Stoker's description of the creature emphasizes animalistic and inhuman features: the long teeth, cruel expression, hairy palms, and so on). But beginning with Bela Lugosi's classic big-screen portrayal of Dracula in 1931, the vampiric image was inflected with sophistication and elegance. These manifestly positive characteristics were augmented in later decades by still more surreal departures from the horrific. Over the last several decades, fictional vampires have rarely been depicted as monsters. Instead, they are romantic antiheroes and social outsiders: author Anne Rice's vampires, those of the teen-oriented *Twilight* stories and films, and the sultry southerners of HBO's *True Blood* stand out in this reformulation. In the *Blade* films and short-lived television series and *Buffy the Vampire Slayer*, protagonists are even promoted to the ranks of superhero.

This metamorphosis of the vampire in popular culture away from horror and toward gothic, romantic heroism is an interesting turn. Unlike zombies, vampires generally embody admired human qualities, among them intelligence, physical beauty, and cultural sophistication. More often than not, they are highly sexualized beings whose capacity to seduce mere mortals is part of their appeal. This is worlds away from the authentic zombie-like vampires of eastern European folklore, which, more often than not, depicts these creatures as feared scavengers, widow-makers, and cradle robbers. Modern media has been responsible for this transformation, but it has flourished because such revised creatures reflect not just human fears but also human desires. The longing for immortal life, beauty, and strength is achieved in vampire fiction, even though it is at a cost—an endless thirst for human blood. Could the enduring appeal of vampires be related to our ambivalence about our own moral standing, as evidenced by the fact that these creatures are at once supernaturally evil and the ideal of what a human life might be?

In contrast to zombies and vampires, ghosts and demons—like angels and saints—enjoy "official" status within a variety of religious institutions in that they are viewed as real—and sometimes dangerous. In popular entertainment, depictions of these range from the fantastical (the beings that maraud Hogwarts castle in J. K. Rowling's widely acclaimed film and book series Harry Potter, for instance) to "realistic" portrayals of spirit possession of human beings. It is on this point that we see a sharp departure from zombie and vampire lore in the popular imagination. While most (not all) concede, however reluctantly, that zombies and vampires don't actually exist, ghosts and demons are often treated as potentially real. This is reinforced in too many horror films to count but also in the past two decades by such "reality" programming as the SyFy Channel's Ghost Hunters and documentary-style films such as The Blair Witch Project (1999) and Paranormal Activity (2007). It is not just reality-style productions that reinforce belief in ghosts but also feature films that are fictional but sufficiently tinged with or inspired by "real" events as to provoke profound dread, where vampire and zombie films might not. In part, this sense of the "uncanny" is provoked by an extensive lack of understanding among the general public of how physics works and therefore how the universe is thought to behave. As one article points out, Albert Einstein's apparently cryptic position that energy cannot be destroyed has been uncritically taken as evidence for the continued existence of our body's energy postmortem (that is, in the form of a "ghost"), but, as any rudimentary familiarity with physics shows, when a person dies, his or her energy goes where all energy from dead organisms goes—back into the environment in the form of heat. Perhaps this decidedly mundane conclusion fails to excite the imagination of the many who simultaneously crave and fear the ongoing existence of the human "person" after death in whatever form it is offered.

The question of ghosts as real phenomena touches on a broader debate and deep-seated cultural anxiety about the status, not just of the deceased but also of the human soul. The differences between souls and ghosts are at best murky and, lacking scientifically acceptable evidence, exist entirely in definitions proffered by popular culture and theology. That the US Christian establishment (especially the larger denominations) embraces the soul but (generally) avoids the question of ghosts speaks to the aspirations of many church organizations to appear rational and modern—a pursuit that encompasses discussion and debate about more than just the uneasy dead.

The 1973 film, *The Exorcist*, for instance, has been prominent in reifying ideas about the demonic in popular culture. In it, we are introduced not solely to the demonic but also the deeply ambivalent orientation of Roman Catholicism toward the demonic. The following example illustrates how the ambivalence of a modern Church to medieval ritual becomes a theological problem that must be solved to save a little girl's life. In one scene, a character named Chris MacNeil is speaking with a Catholic priest, Father Damien Karras, about her daughter, Regan. MacNeil is at her wit's end and, though not religious, has approached a priest for help when modern medical science and psychology seem to have failed. The problem, she explains, is that Regan has apparently been possessed by an evil spirit. At first hesitant, MacNeil confesses her hope that Karras might arrange an exorcism to drive the demon away and so cure her daughter. Dumbfounded, Karras explains that she probably knows as much as he about exorcism and that to do things properly, they would have to invent a time machine and travel back to the sixteenth century! Her turn to be surprised; MacNeil is incredulous. Since when do Catholic priests not know how to perform exorcisms? Ever since, Karras explains patiently, the world learned about mental illness and anxiety disorders.

This tension within the modern Catholic Church between scientific rationalism and an undercurrent of conviction in the real existence of the devil and his minions—and ghosts too—provides a dramatic backdrop against which the plot of *The Exorcist* advances. In the broader context of Western culture, this question has a quality of seriousness to it that is absent from considerations of zombies and vampires. Demons, demonic forces, and the ghostly dead are at least considered as *possibly* real, and this is reflected in the sober tenor of how such creatures are portrayed—even in film and fiction.

The articles in Part Four approach these phenomena from several vantages. In the media-driven cacophony of perspectives and questions, convictions and fears, about ghosts, vampires, and zombies, students of such phenomena might well ask whether supernatural beings like these have now transcended their own fictionalization to become culturally real in a way that will shape religious and otherworldly knowledge and awareness in decades to come.

The Science (and Non-Science) of Ghosts

By Benjamin Radford

G HOSTS ARE EVERYWHERE—YET NOWHERE. CULTURES all around the world believe in spirits that survive death to dwell in another realm. In fact, ghosts are among the most widely believed in paranormal phenomena: millions of people are interested in ghosts, and a 2019 Ipsos/YouGov poll found that 45 percent of Americans say that ghosts "definitely or probably exist."

The idea that the dead remain with us in spirit is ancient and appears in countless stories from the Bible to *Macbeth*. It even spawned a folklore genre: ghost stories. Belief in ghosts is part of a larger web of related paranormal beliefs, including near-death experience, life after death, and spirit communication. Such beliefs offer many people comfort—who doesn't want to believe that our departed loved ones are looking out for us or are with us in times of need?

Many people have tried to—or claimed to—communicate with spirits over the centuries; in Victorian England, for example, it was fashionable for upper-crust ladies to hold séances in their parlors after tea with friends. So-called Ghost Clubs dedicated to searching for ghostly evidence formed at prestigious universities, including Cambridge and Oxford, and in 1882, the most prominent such organization, the Society for Psychical Research, was established. Eleanor Sidgwick was an investigator (and later president) of that group and could be considered the world's first female ghostbuster. Meanwhile across the pond, during the late 1800s, many American psychics claimed to speak to the dead—and were exposed as frauds by skeptical investigators such as Harry Price and Harry Houdini.

Despite these early, sporadic spirit investigation attempts, it wasn't until recently that ghost hunting became a widespread interest around the world. Much of this is due to the popular TV series *Ghost Hunters*, which ended 13 seasons without finding good evidence of ghosts. The show spawned dozens of spin-offs and imitators, and it's not hard to see why the show was so popular: the premise is that anyone can look for ghosts. The two original stars were ordinary guys (plumbers, in fact) who decided to look for evidence of spirits. Their message: You don't need to be an egghead scientist—or even have any training in science or investigation—to look for ghosts. All you need is some free time, a dark place, and a few cameras and gadgets. If you look long enough (and your threshold of evidence is low enough), any "unexplained" light or noise could be evidence of ghosts.

The Science and Logic of Ghosts

Scientifically evaluating ghosts is problematic for several reasons, including that surprisingly diverse phenomena are attributed to ghosts. To one person a door closing on its own is a sign of a ghost, while for others, it may be missing keys, a faint scent, a cold area in a home, or even a dream about a dead friend. When sociologists Dennis and Michele Waskul interviewed ghost experiencers for their 2016 book *Ghostly Encounters: The Hauntings of Everyday Life* (Temple University Press) they found that "many participants were not sure that they had encountered a ghost and remained uncertain that such phenomena were even possible, simply because they did not see something that approximated the conventional image of a 'ghost.' Instead, many of our respondents were simply convinced that they had experienced something uncanny—something inexplicable, extraordinary, mysterious, or eerie." Because of this, many people claiming to have had a ghostly experience didn't necessarily see anything that most people would recognize as a classic "ghost." In fact, they may have had totally different experiences whose only common factor is that it was not easily explained.

Ghost research is greatly complicated by the fact that there's no consensus about what a ghost is—even among ghost hunters and "experts." Some believe, for example, that ghosts are spirits of the dead who get "lost" on their way to "the other side"; others are sure that ghosts are instead telepathic entities projected into the world or strong emotions somehow recorded and later "replayed" in the environment (often called "stone tape theory"). Still others create their own categories for different types of ghosts, such as poltergeists, residual hauntings, intelligent spirits, and shadow people. It's a fun exercise in fantasy, but, of course, it's all made up, like speculating on different types of dragons; there are as many types of ghosts as you want there to be.

There are many contradictions inherent in ideas about ghosts. For example, are ghosts material or not? Either they can move through walls and solid objects without disturbing them, or they can slam doors shut and throw objects across a room. According to logic (not to mention the laws of physics), it's one or the other. If ghosts are human souls, why do they appear clothed and with inanimate objects such as hats and dresses—not to mention the many reports of ghost trains, cars, and carriages? If instead ghosts are the result of unavenged deaths, why are there unsolved murders since ghosts are said to communicate with psychic mediums and should be able to identify their killers for the police? And so on—just about any claim about ghosts raises logical reasons to doubt it.

Ghost hunters use many creative (and dubious) methods to detect ghostly presences, including psychics. Most ghost hunters claim to be scientific and give that appearance because they use high-tech scientific equipment such as Geiger counters, electromagnetic field detectors, and infrared cameras. Yet none of this equipment has ever been shown to actually detect ghosts. Centuries ago, people believed that flames turned blue in the presence of ghosts. Few people today believe that bit of ghost lore, but it's likely that many of the signs taken as evidence by modern ghost hunters will be seen as just as silly and quaint centuries from now.

Many ghost hunters claim that ghosts haven't been proven real because we don't yet have the right technology to detect the spirit world. But this, too, can't be true: either ghosts exist and appear in our ordinary physical world and visible spectrum (and can, therefore, be detected and recorded in photographs, film, and video), or they don't. If ghosts exist and can be scientifically detected or recorded, then we should find hard evidence of that—yet we don't. If ghosts exist but cannot be scientifically recorded, then that means that all the photos, videos, audio, and other recordings claimed to be ghosts are not in fact ghosts. With so many contradictions—and so little science brought to bear—it's not surprising that despite the efforts of thousands of ghost hunters for decades, no hard evidence of ghosts has been found.

Why Many Believe

Much of the belief in ghosts comes not only from television shows but also from some personal experiences. Maybe the person grew up in a home where the presence of a spirit was taken for granted. Maybe they had some unnerving experience on a ghost tour or at a local haunt. But still, they believe, science has offered a logical, physical rationale for ghosts. It is widely claimed that Albert Einstein himself proved the possibility of ghosts with his First Law of Thermodynamics: If energy cannot be created or destroyed but only change form, then what happens to our bodies' energy when we die? Could that somehow reappear as a ghost?

The idea seems superficially reasonable—unless you understand basic physics. The answer is simple and not at all mysterious. After a person dies, the body's energy goes where all organisms' energy goes after death: into the environment. The energy is released in the form of heat, and the body is transferred into the animals that eat us (i.e., wild animals if unburied, or worms if we are interred, or heat if we're cremated), and the plants that absorb us. There is no bodily "energy" that survives death.

While legions of amateur ghost hunters imagine (and portray) themselves as on the cutting edge of ghost research, they are engaging in what folklorists call ostension or legend tripping, a form of playacting in which people "act out" an existing narrative or legend, often involving ghosts or supernatural elements. In his book *Aliens, Ghosts, and Cults:*

Legends We Live (University Press of Mississippi, 2003) folklorist Bill Ellis notes that ghost hunters take the search seriously and "venture out to challenge supernatural beings, confront them in consciously dramatized form, then return to safety.... The stated purpose of such activities is not entertainment but a sincere effort to test and define boundaries of the 'real' world." It's a fun and fascinating hobby but not an investigation or research.

In the end, it doesn't matter what all the scientists, skeptics, and ghost hunters think. If ghosts are real and are some sort of as-yet-unknown energy, then their existence will (like all other scientific findings) sooner or later be discovered and verified by scientists through controlled experiments—not by weekend ghost hunters wandering around abandoned houses late at night with cameras and flashlights.

Despite mountains of ambiguous photos, sounds, and videos, the evidence of ghosts is no better today than it was a year ago, a decade ago, or a century ago. There are two possible reasons for the failure of ghost hunters to find good evidence of their quarry. The first is that ghosts don't exist and that reports of ghosts can be explained by psychology, misperceptions, mistakes, and hoaxes. The second option is that ghosts *do* exist but that ghost hunters are simply incompetent and need to bring more scientific rigor to the search because what they've done so far has clearly failed.

Ghost hunting is not really about the evidence (if it were, the search would have been abandoned long ago). Instead, it's about having fun with friends, telling spooky stories, and the enjoyment of pretending they're searching the edge of the unknown. After all, everyone loves a good ghost story.

Why Zombies Have Taken Over Pop Culture

By Chris Longridge

W HAT'S THAT COMING OVER THE HILL, is it a monster? No. More of a shuffling horde of reanimated corpses, actually. Dead men walking. Z-heads.

You may have noticed that zombies are quite popular these days—in the last five years alone we've seen variations on the theme in *The Walking Dead* (and spin-off *Fear the Walking Dead*), *iZombie*, *Game of Thrones*, *World War Z*, *Dead Snow*, *Warm Bodies*, *Maggie*, *Cell*, *The Girl With All The Gifts*, *Pride And Prejudice And Zombies*, *Scouts Guide To The Zombie Apocalypse*, *Cockneys vs Zombies*, *Pro-Wrestlers vs Zombies* (yep) and, lest we forget, *Zombeavers*.

And that's just the tip of the undead iceberg. They're everywhere—in video games, in comedies, on children's T-shirts, in jokes ("What do vegan zombies eat? Graaaaaaains") … You can even see space zombies in Doctor Who this week. They're coming to get you, Barbara!

But why so many? And why now?

The Dead Begin Rising from the Grave

Prevailing wisdom says that the modern preoccupation with zombies began with George Romero's low-budget shocker from 1968, *Night of the Living Dead*. Well yes, up to a point, but also no, not at all. The earliest zombie movie was in fact a full *36* years earlier, Edward Halperin's *White Zombie* in 1932. (It spawned a sequel, *Revolt of the Zombies*, in 1936.)

Dozens more followed over the subsequent three decades, though admittedly their bad guy of choice was more the voodoo-inspired "mindless henchman"-type than your actual walking corpse.

Romero certainly set the template for the modern zombie, though, for which he borrowed heavily from Richard Matheson's novel *I Am Legend*. The zombie as we know it is a lumbering dead person, lacking all but the most basic motor skills, reanimated by mysterious means (usually a virus, sometimes of extra-terrestrial origin) and intent only on feeding on the flesh of the living.

Zombie movies continued as a sub-genre of horror for the next three decades, combining traditional scares with social comment about racism, consumerism and conformity. But it wasn't until the millennium that the undead horde reached a tipping point and went mainstream.

Zombies Take Over the World

And this time, they were quick off the starting blocks. *Resident Evil (2002)*, *28 Days Later (2002)* and Zack Snyder's *Dawn of the Dead* remake (2004) rebooted the genre by giving it a shot of speed. Though highly cinematic, the fast-moving zombie (or "infected", depending on the franchise) dispenses with satirical nuance in favour of thrills—nothing wrong with that, just a different flavour for a different audience.

But the Romero zombie wasn't dead—so to speak.

Shaun of the Dead (2004) gave it a sentimental comedy twist, and Romero made a comeback of sorts after 20 years with *Land of the Dead* (in which *Shaun* creators Simon Pegg and Edgar Wright made a brief cameo).

Author Max Brooks set out the most comprehensive definition of the "modern" zombie in his *Zombie Survival Guide*, and expanded upon it in his hit 2006 novel *World War Z: An Oral History Of The Zombie War*, upon which the Brad Pitt movie was barely based at all.

Then came *The Walking Dead*—first a comic-book series following the Romero formula, later the second-most-watched TV show *in the world*. (No. 1 is *Game of Thrones*, which has its own shambling horde of frozen undead.)

After that, the fences collapsed and the undead came swarming into the gated community of mainstream culture.

The Center For Disease Control, which actually features in The Walking Dead, produced a special blog of their own in 2011, *Preparedness 101: Zombie Apocalypse* as a "fun new way of teaching the importance of emergency preparedness".

Junior officers in the US Department of Defence even drafted a comprehensive fictional plan for dealing with a zombie invasion as a means of practicing DoD strategic planning. (Some conspiracy theorists even appear to believe it is real.)

But what is it about zombies that appeals to us right *now*?

Well, we'd argue there are a few reasons for the rise of the undead ...

What Does a Zombie *Mean*, Culturally?

The first reason is straightforward and uncontroversial—it's even baked into Romero's oeuvre. As well as being scary and gross like all good monsters, the zombie is an incredibly versatile metaphor.

Night of the Living Dead, with its decisive black hero and cowardly Bourgeois White Dad figure, was as counter-cultural as they came. The (white) snipers ranged across the horizon in the closing scenes were indistinguishable from a shambling row of zombies. In 1978, *Dawn of the Dead* famously took aim at the aimless crowds of shoppers who pollinate malls across the world.

The undead have at times been argued to represent the underclass, as in *Land of the Dead*, communism and fears of globalisation. In one controversial snippet at the beginning of Zack Snyder's *Dawn of the Dead*, the director even appeared to be drawing a parallel with Muslims at prayer (it would be disingenuous to claim that Snyder, so soon on the tails of 9/11, wasn't making some kind of point, however incoherent).

Then of course there's The Big One. As Simon Pegg put it, "Where their pointy-toothed cousins are all about sex and bestial savagery, the zombie trumps all by personifying our deepest fear: **death**. Zombies are our destiny writ large. Slow and steady in their approach, weak, clumsy, often absurd, the zombie relentlessly closes in, unstoppable, intractable."

You can use zombies to take potshots at mortality, government ineptitude, bioengineering and unchecked technological advance, slavery, capitalism, exploitation, social division, anything you like. It's no coincidence that a common, contemporary image of the zombie apocalypse is a hand-held camera viewing a surging crowd of civilians and soldiers, shot in a modern city with fireballs and black smoke in the sky: it's the *news*, made palatable by its fantasy context.

But it's not that simple. In fact, it's even simpler.

Because simplicity is the appeal of the zombie. They don't have complex motivations, they don't have a goal, they don't have an arc. They seek out the living and they eat them, that's all they do. Kill them or they'll eat you.

They're not even the real antagonists of the stories they occupy, they're just a means to an end—what they do is cut to the heart of our human problems by stripping civilisation down to the bare essentials. When there are enough of them, society collapses. Humanity's web of intricate nuances—all the noise of social networks, political compromise, corporate hierarchy, conflicting identities, faceless terror threats and branded infotainment—it all collapses too, and we're left with some really simple questions.

In fact, *The Walking Dead* asks those very questions on the back of each volume of the comic:

The question we cannot help but ask when watching a zombie movie is: "What would I do, if that were me?"

In this way, the zombie movie occupies the same place in the movie-going psyche that the Western used to. The post-apocalyptic landscape is one of isolated communities and no rule of law, where strong men (almost always men) can terrorise the weak with impunity, and faith in blood and friendship is all that keeps anarchy at bay. Where the infinite gradations of "right" and "wrong" come down to kill or be killed.

In the internet era, where long, complacently-held values are challenged by a billion different voices every day, a story that filters out the static has enormous appeal.

Zombie stories allow us to ask, free of confusion and doubt, "Who am I?"

A 'Vampire's' Remains Were Found about 30 Years Ago. Now DNA Is Giving Him New Life.

By Michael E. Ruane

H E HAD BEEN IN HIS GRAVE so long that when his family dug him up to burn his heart, the organ had decomposed and was not there.

Desperate to stop him from stalking them, they took his head and limbs and rearranged them on top of his ribs in the design of a skull and crossbones. He was a "vampire," after all, and in rural New England in the early 1800s, this was how you dealt with them.

When they were finished, they reburied him in his stone-lined grave and replaced the wooden coffin lid, on which someone had used brass tacks to form the inscription "JB 55," for his initials and his age.

Now, 200 years or so after the death of what has become the country's best-studied "vampire," DNA sleuths have tracked down his probable name: John Barber.

He was probably a hard-working farmer. Missing his top front teeth, he was no neck biter. He had a broken collar bone that had not healed right and an arthritic knee that may have made him limp, and he had died an awful death, probably from tuberculosis, which was so bad it had scarred his ribs.

The latest findings in a case that started in 1990 when his coffin was discovered in a gravel quarry in Griswold, Conn., are contained in a new report by, among others, experts at the Armed Forces Medical Examiner System's DNA laboratory in Dover, Del.

The report was summarized in a presentation on July 23 at the National Museum of Health and Medicine in Silver Spring, which aided the study and is where the remains are held.

The case is unusual because Barber may be the country's only supposed "vampire" whose bones have been studied by scientists.

"This case has been a mystery since the 1990s," Charla Marshall said in an email. Marshall is a forensic scientist with SNA International in Alexandria, Va., who worked on the project. "Now that we have expanded technological capabilities, we wanted to revisit JB 55 to see whether we could solve the mystery of who he was."

It is the latest chapter in a project that has cast light on the eerie vampire scare in New England—Connecticut and Rhode Island especially—in the late 1700s and early 1800s, and its connection to the spread of tuberculosis, or "consumption," as it was called.

The highly contagious disease was so wasting and terrifying that those who died of it were believed to leave their graves, infecting relatives and draining away blood and life, scholars have said.

These attacks were more mysterious and less graphic than those of the bloodsucking vampires of Gothic fiction.

"This was not ... bats flying through the night," said Nicholas F. Bellantoni, the retired Connecticut state archaeologist who worked on the case from the start and is one of the report's authors. "This is not Bela Lugosi."

The terror they brought was real. Consumption often caused a bloody cough and left victims pale and gaunt with blood in the corners of their mouths, author and folklorist Michael E. Bell wrote.

"The emaciated figure strikes one with terror," recounted an 18th-century doctor quoted by Bell in a 2013 essay in the journal Kritikos. "The forehead covered with drops of sweat. The cheeks ... a livid crimson. The eyes sunk. ... The breath offensive, quick and laborious."

The vampire's true menace seemed to come after death, and he had to be killed again during what Bell called "therapeutic exhumation." Often the suspected vampire was a family member who had died of the disease and was thought to be infecting sons, daughters or a wife.

Family members were frequently the ones conducting the exhumation. Bell has documented 80 such cases, mostly in remote areas of New England.

"This was being done out of fear and out of love," Bellantoni said. "People were dying in their families, and they had no way of stopping it, and just maybe this was what could stop the deaths. ... They didn't want to do this, but they wanted to protect those that were still living."

The best method of killing the suspected vampire was to check the exhumed corpse to see whether any liquid blood remained in the heart. If so, the deceased was probably a vampire, according to the belief. The heart was then removed and burned, with family members sometimes inhaling the smoke to prevent further disease.

Similar incidents have long turned up in Europe, where there are many accounts of corpses being dug up, burned, rearranged, decapitated or having stakes driven through them.

In Barber's case, there was probably no heart to burn, Bellantoni and Paul S. Sledzik wrote in 1994. So "the bones of the chest were disrupted" and the skull and thigh bones were "placed in a 'skull and cross bones' position," they wrote.

After Barber's grave was discovered, his remains were sent to the museum for study, and a sample from a thigh bone was sent to the DNA lab for analysis. The technology of 30 years ago yielded scant results, the paper's authors wrote, and identification was impossible.

When modern tools were used—Y-chromosomal DNA profiling and surname prediction via genealogy data available on the Internet—the experts said they came up with a match for the last name: Barber.

They then checked old cemetery and newspaper records to see whether any Barbers ever lived in Griswold.

They discovered a newspaper notice mentioning the death there in 1826 of a 12-year-old boy named Nathan Barber, whose father was a John Barber. Researchers had found a grave near JB's containing a coffin with the notation "NB 13" similarly tacked on the lid.

The project began in November 1990 when an abandoned cemetery was encountered during mining at a sand and gravel facility in Griswold, according to a study by Sledzik, Bellantoni and colleague David A. Poirier.

Human skeletons and crumbling coffin parts emerged from the Earth, and two human skulls tumbled down an embankment when three boys playing there dislodged them.

Investigators eventually removed the remains of 27 people—five men, eight women and 14 children—from 28 graves in what scholars discovered was an old burying ground called the Walton Family Cemetery. (One grave contained evidence of a coffin but no human remains.)

It was grave No. 4 that drew the most attention.

"Every one was in good anatomical position ... except this one individual, JB 55," Bellantoni said.

Under his coffin lid, Bellantoni and his colleagues found the strange skull-and-crossbones arrangement.

"His thigh bones ... were uprooted from the anatomical position and crossed over the chest," he said.

"The chest had been broken into, and the ... skull was decapitated and moved away," he said. "I was totally befuddled. I had no clue what I was looking at."

Research soon suggested a link to the New England vampire folk belief, he said.

"So JB turned out to have tuberculosis ... [evident] because of the lesions on his ribs," he said. "We do believe that he was rearranged in the grave because he was believed to be undead."

Bellantoni said JB had probably been deceased four or five years when he was exhumed, which, based on his recovered coffin hardware, probably happened in the early 1800s.

"Here in New England ... we had large farming families," he said. "Because they didn't understand the transmission of the disease, you had family members who were suffering from tuberculosis sitting at the dinner table with the whole family coughing, and you had tubercular victims sleeping in one room with five or six brothers and sisters coughing.

"It was epidemic," he said.

So what now of poor John Barber, the alleged vampire?

"Listen," Bellantoni said. "He was a hard-working farmer. Probably lower-middle class. ... You could see it in his bones. You could see it in the arthritic condition of his vertebrae. ... Hard-, hard-working. Good Christian man, I am sure."

The Health and Legal Concerns of Modern Vampires

By Jarryd Bartle

V AMPIRES WALK AMONG US.
According to researcher Dr John Edgar Browning, from the Georgia Institute of Technology, real-life vampirism is a growing blood-drinking subculture worthy of academic attention.

Indeed, although they may not transform into bats or hold the secret to immortality, a vampire subculture has been well documented in Australia since at least the 1990s.

Here is everything you need to know to satisfy your bloodlust.

Wait, What?

The origins of the modern vampiric lifestyle can be traced back to the early S&M and goth scenes of the 1970s, which attracted quirky individuals interested in the darker side of life. However, modern vampirism didn't quite gain a cohesive identity until blood fetishists, new age spiritualists and cosplayers started talking online and creating their own vampiric mythos.

According to Sanguinarius.org, one of the longest running online resources for the vampire subculture, real-life vampires feel a desire or need to consume blood or—in its more spiritual variant—absorb "psychic energy" from willing donors.

The subculture is a broad tent encompassing individuals who see consuming blood as a health need, a sexual kink, a lifestyle choice and a deeper spiritual yearning.

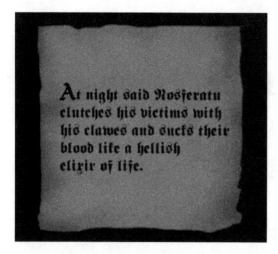

At night said Nosferatu clutches his victims with his clawes and sucks their blood life a hellish elixir of life.

Real-life vampires have always had some presence down under, with media attention waxing and waning depending on the latest film releases—we got a lot of 'real-life vampire' stories at the peak of *Twilight* for example.

However, very little attention has been paid to the health and legal considerations of the subculture.

Is This Safe?

It will come as no surprise that blood consumption doesn't exactly have glowing support by health authorities.

Along with the risk of blood-borne virus transmission, biting or even surgically cutting the skin of a willing donor carries the risk of scarring, infection or even death if not done correctly.

The blood itself isn't very dangerous, consisting of mostly water with a bit of protein thrown in. The only potential hazard is if you consume too much iron, the one significant nutritional component of the sanguine fluid.

Real-life vampires mitigate health risks by screening donors for transmissible disease, using sterile tools to lancet blood and by limiting the amount of blood consumed to a couple of spoonfuls.

Whilst having a quirky habit like blood drinking isn't necessarily an indication of mental illness, a psychiatric condition called Renfield's syndrome (or clinical vampirism) has been documented if behaviour becomes obsessive or harmful.

If blood drinking is compulsive or is coupled with delusions of grandeur that you are Dracula once the sun goes down, it may be time to seek help from a professional.

Is This Legal?

The vampire subculture prides itself on ensuring (often written) consent of donors before bloodletting—but consent will not always act as a defence to criminal charges where actual injury or death occurs.

Vampires have tried to negate legal risks by establishing a Donor Bill of Rights, to provide for the safety and well-being of donors. However, it's unlikely these guidelines would protect someone being prosecuted for inflicting injury or—if something were to go horribly wrong—murder.

Things get even more complicated from a legal perspective if money is exchanging hands. It is possible that paying to drink someone's blood could be considered a form of sex work: triggering a number of specialist regulatory regimes, often backed by criminal offences if not complied with.

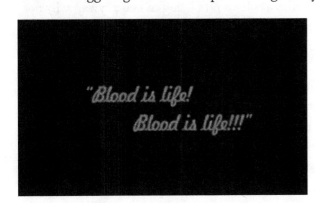

"Blood is life!
Blood is life!!!"

So unlike an Anne Rice novel, vampirism in the real world comes with a number of health and legal considerations.

It's important that burgeoning blood-suckers know all the risks before biting down on their next meal.

Here's the Safest Hideout in a Zombie Apocalypse, According to Statistics

By Myles Gough

I N THE EVENT OF A ZOMBIE apocalypse, it's imperative that you have a plan. If you're influenced by the movies, then you might be inclined to take your chances and head for the nearest pub or shopping mall in order to outwit a growing horde of bloodthirsty zombies.

Your average shopping mall is equipped with all the important first-world amenities we desire. And if the whole world's going to hell anyway, why not live out your days eating cheap fast food and trying on clothing you'd never be able to afford in real life? And at least in a pub you can get blind drunk while you wait for the inevitable.

But if your ultimate aim is survival, neither option is *that* good, unless, of course, you manage to discover a pub or mall in the middle of nowhere.

In 2015, in an effort to better understand the spread of real diseases, a team of statisticians from Cornell University in the US modelled the spread of a fictitious zombie plague travelling across the continental United States.

Their results indicated that the best place to avoid infection is in remote, sparsely populated locations.

The authors explained the Northern Rocky Mountains—probably somewhere in Montana or in Canada—would be the absolute best place to hide.

Apparently, a full-scale zombie outbreak in New York City could take a month or so to reach upstate New York, due to geographic distance and a slowing rate of infection, which means you'd have a decent amount of time to plot your escape to the sticks.

"Given the dynamics of the disease, once the zombies invade more sparsely populated areas, the whole outbreak slows down—there are fewer humans to bite, so you start creating zombies at a slower rate," lead author Alex Alemi said in a press statement at the time.

In their model, cities—predictably—fall fast. Just imagine a zombie attack on a crowded New York City subway. Horrifying, right? But their modelling shows it would take weeks for the outbreak to reach rural communities, and months to reach the northern mountain time zone.

Of course, if movies have taught us anything, not all zombies are created equally. Depending on how freakishly fast they are, or how well they can climb, you may need to revise your estimates.

As they explained in a press statement when the study was first published," the project was an overview of modern epidemiology modeling, starting with differential equations to model a fully connected population, then moving on to lattice-based models, and ending with a full US-scale simulation of an outbreak across the continental US."

The simulation had to account for a population of roughly 300 million people, with each person presumed to be in one of four states: human, infected, zombie, and dead zombie.

It tracked the spread of the epidemic by modelling the random interactions between these people—for instance, zombie bites leading to infection, and humans killing zombies, delaying the spread. In the end the researchers were able to pinpoint locations where the disease would take longest to reach.

Even with optimal hideouts, however, the outlook for Americans is pretty bad, should a zombie plague actually materialise.

"We ... discover that for 'realistic' parameters, we are largely doomed," the authors concluded in their paper's abstract.

It may seem a bit silly to simulate a zombie outbreak, but the US Pentagon and the US Centers for Disease Control have both used zombie outbreak-scenarios to help develop training programs for disaster readiness.

And, you know, as a contingency plan for when it actually happens.

Discussion Questions

1. In what ways do amateur "ghost hunters" attempt to prove the existence of ghosts and spirits? In your view, do these efforts constitute scientific investigation? Do you find the "evidence" persuasive? Why or why not?

2. Are ideas about vampires taken seriously in the United States or is this merely a form of popular entertainment? Why do you think these stories are appealing to people?

3. Who are the "real" vampires in the contemporary United States? How do they mark themselves as a community? How do they see themselves as different from other people? What are their primary concerns in a society that openly trivializes their subculture?

4. The zombie has been characterized as "an incredibly versatile metaphor." Do you agree with this characterization? In what ways have zombies been used as a basis for social commentary, and do you find such analogizing persuasive?

5. Do you believe that widespread interest in zombies has socially positive functions? If so, what are they?

Further Readings

Bishop, Kyle William. *American Zombie Gothic: The Rise and Fall (and Rise) of the Walking Dead in Popular Culture*. Jefferson, NC: McFarland and Company, 2010.

In this blend of academics and popular writing, literary scholar Bishop explores the world of zombies as a powerful undercurrent in US ideas and fantasy concerning the transcendent, especially in popular culture and cinema. His analysis begins with the slave-era African/ Caribbean foundations of the zombie idea and culminates in the postmodern zombie of multiple genres of popular entertainment.

Boluk, Stephanie, and Wylie Lenz, eds. *Generation Zombie: Essays on the Living Dead in Modern Culture*. Jefferson, NC: McFarland and Company, 2011.

A recent collection of academic essays (mainly from the fields of cultural and media studies) that explore the rise of cinematic and cultural zombies and the living dead as related to a variety of issues, including US imperialism, environmentalism, race, class, and digital technologies.

Clements, Susannah. *The Vampire Defanged: How the Embodiment of Evil Became a Romantic Hero*. Grand Rapids, MI: Brazos Press, 2011.

Clements's analysis of the shifting cultural roles of the vampire from monstrous terror to romantic teenage antihero and beyond. Her study may be of special interest to some Christians, as she writes from an explicitly faith-based vantage. Nevertheless, Clements's exploration is a careful, nonpolemic one that has particularly strong insight into the historical relationship between Christianity and vampire mythology.

Davis, Wade. *The Serpent and the Rainbow: A Harvard Scientist's Astonishing Journey into the Secret Societies of Haitian Voodoo, Zombies, and Magic*. New York: Touchstone Books, 1997.

In this now-classic (though still controversial in some quarters) ethnographic detective story, anthropologist Davis seeks to discover the cultural and pharmacological foundations of the zombie phenomenon in Haiti. Fascinating and extremely well written, the true value of Davis's text lies in its elegant and poignant exploration of the rich tapestry of Haitian Vodou. Not all students of ethnobotany (study of the cultural use of plants) agree with his conclusions, but Davis's study (first published in the early 1980s) had a deep effect on the scholarly study of African Caribbean magic and witchcraft that still resonates in the twenty-first century.

Ellis, Bill. *Aliens, Ghosts, and Cults: Legends We Live*. Jackson: University Press of Mississippi, 2003.

Ellis provides a perspective from cultural studies on the psychology and motivations behind narratives and legends of the paranormal, especially in terms of how they form a basis for social solidarity within communities of believers.

Hufford, David J. *The Terror that Comes at Night: An Experience-Centered Study of Supernatural Assault Traditions*. Philadelphia: University of Pennsylvania Press, 1989.

In this folkloric analysis, Hufford investigates the psychology, culture, and experience behind the "Old Hag" tradition of haunting—a phenomenon that is surprisingly frequent and ubiquitous across societies.

Jenkins, Mark Collins. *Vampire Forensics: Uncovering the Origins of an Enduring Legend*. Washington, DC: National Geographic, 2010.

Jenkins's book provides nonspecialist readers with a solid introduction to both the cultural and scientific aspects behind vampire beliefs. In particular, his examination of anthropological examples of similar ideas from unrelated social and language groups, and his study of archaeological evidence that in some cases dates back thousands of years, provides an insightful and comprehensive window onto the social functions of vampire myths across human societies.

McNally, Raymond T., and Radu Florescu. *In Search of Dracula: The History of Dracula and Vampires*. New York: Mariner Books, 1994.

This historical biography should be of interest to anyone wishing to understand the foundations of Irish novelist Bram Stoker's fictional character, Count Dracula. In their work, McNally and Florescu document the life and times of fifteenth-century Romanian despot Vlad Tepes III, "son of Dracul," and widely known as "the Impaler." In so doing, the authors' careful analysis of the historical record paints a portrait of the original Dracula that makes his fictional descendent seem rather tame by comparison.;

Waskul, Denis, and Michele Waskul. *Ghostly Encounters: The Hauntings of Everyday Life*. Philadelphia: Temple University Press, 2016.

A sociological and ethnographical investigation of hauntings and ghosts among Midwestern Americans. In particular, the authors seek to deconstruct the transformation of uncanny or unsettling experiences into ghost narrative and belief.

Part V

||||||||||||||||||||||||||||||||||||||||||||||||||||||||||||||||||||||||||||||||||||||||||||||||||||||||||||||||||||||||||||||||||||||||||||||||||||||||||||||||||||||

Fear in the Witching Hour

Introduction

Among the most popular courses in colleges around the United States are those that delve into the mysterious phenomena of witchcraft. Frequently, such courses are instructed as part of nonspecialist general education or introductory-level curricula within departments of anthropology, history, or religious studies. While most students who enroll in these courses have no intention of pursuing careers in these disciplines, the abiding preoccupation among "modern" university students with supernatural forces taken to be sinister or malevolent is a curious fact that demands explanation.

If we ask "average" Americans what they imagine is meant by the terms "witches" and "witchcraft," most people are unlikely to respond in terms of such abstractions. Rather, Americans raised from the post–Second World War baby boomer culture and later draw on images of the witch coming in equal measures from biblical exposition, classic literature, historical stereotypes, Halloween kitsch, and more recent strains of popular culture (especially in cinema and television). In the Bible, the notorious Witch of Endor (First Book of Samuel, chapter 28:3–25) provides a fitting nemesis for contemporary "Bible-believing" Christians (at least 28 percent of US adults, according to the 2014 Gallup Values and Beliefs poll). But even if one isn't exposed from the pulpit to a naturalized vision of the evil-doing hag, the canon of English literature features a triad of similar creatures immortalized by William Shakespeare in his play *Macbeth*. The "weird sisters" of Shakespeare's imagination were most immediately inspired by the contemporary work of historian Raphael Holinshed on Great Britain and

Ireland in the late sixteenth century. They were doubtless also grounded in widespread medieval and early modern fears of Christian society under attack—from raging epidemics and undiagnosed disease, the distant yet terrifying specter of Islam, the unpredictable ebb and flow of natural disasters (for instance, earthquakes, floods, crop blights, sudden deep freezes), and—from the late fifteenth century if not before—the mutual demonization of Christian sects within Europe itself and the devastating wars this internal conflict spurred. The legacy of the 1692 Salem persecutions and images of the witch drawn from these sources (of which more are offered next) have been supplemented by popular culture that seems endlessly obsessed with witchcraft as entertainment—from the popular television series *Bewitched* and *Charmed* to *The Wizard of Oz*, *The Blair Witch Project*, and the Harry Potter series of books and films. These strands of culture have at least two things in common: (1) that the line between how Americans define magic as opposed to witchcraft is easily blurred and (2) that the status of witches as malevolent, antisocial agents is hotly contested.

At this point, we need a definition (at least a provisional one) of our key term—witchcraft. Historically, scholars have employed the term to refer to transcendent power manipulated by human beings in order to cause *harm* in the world—most especially by plaguing human beings with misfortune and suffering in one form or another (for example, natural disasters or epidemics). Witchcraft can be analytically distinguished from the related term "sorcery" on the grounds that the former involves a general belief in the logic of unseen forces, while the latter entails such a belief *and* (typically) secret ritualized activity on the part of a knowledgeable agent, or sorcerer. Although this definition is not universally accepted and thus always subject to revision, it does represent a reasonable cross-section of anthropological opinion on witchcraft as a social institution—at least as this body of activity is imagined, interpreted, and valorized across various scales of the social community (from the local to the national and beyond). What it does *not* represent, however, are ideas and practices devised and put into action by a variety of contemporary new religions whose members are self-styled modern witches. For these, witchcraft power denotes a distinctive perspective on both nature and the universe (as repositories of cosmic energies and powers) and the Self, which is considered by some to be a wellspring or node of creative energies drawn from the universe at large. Because these latter groups generally view witchcraft as the outcome of rich, life-affirming insights, the traditional definition of witchcraft as harmful magic fails to capture the full scope of interpretation that attends a twenty-first-century religious landscape.

In Part Five, the selections have accordingly less to do with witchcraft as a type of ritual or religious activity per se and more to do with competing values and interpretations that saturate a national marketplace of religious possibilities in American society. On the one hand, there remains an abiding and widespread fear of witches and the powers they are said to embody, particularly among traditional religious authorities and believers. According to most anthropologists, social historians, and others, it is this fear—and the anxiety it generates—that accounts for the majority of witchcraft beliefs around the world. As these articles demonstrate, it is the *idea* of witchcraft (rather than objective cadres of flesh-and-blood persons and the actions they take) that provokes both concern and enthusiasm, depending on who one listens to. This begs the question of *why?* Why does witchcraft appear at all as a form of explanation, and why, given an abundance of reasoned evidence, do people continue to believe?

Whether one valorizes witchcraft as socially positive or negative, this question can be partially answered (albeit indirectly) by way of the continuing cultural fascination with the 1692 legal and cultural persecutions of "witches" that took place in Salem, Massachusetts—among the most famous dramas of colonial America. It is easy to overgeneralize a complex set of events, but the outlines of this episode involved a number of adolescent girls from an initially small number of farming families in Salem Village (modern Danvers) experiencing a variety of physiological symptoms that, by the standards of the time, defied easy medical explanation. These included spontaneous paralysis, visions, glossolalia (speaking in tongues), and animal mimicry. In the absence of medical explanation, Salem residents (chief among them the community pastor) proposed that a conspiracy of Satan-inspired witches lay at the heart of the girls' torment. Over the spring and summer months of 1692, an ever-widening circle of the accused were arrested. All of these, oddly enough, either fit a well-established profile of what witches were said to be like or were at odds with the victims' families, the Salem pastor, and the pastor's allies. Of these, over 20 ultimately died—most were hanged, but one man was tortured to death and several others died in prison awaiting trial.

These, then, are the general circumstances surrounding the persecutions. Social historians have long suspected that, whatever the views of Salem residents, explanation for the episode could be found not so much in the diabolical but in the entanglement of social and cultural forces. Whereas the earliest English residents of the Massachusetts colony are believed to have shared a general vision of New England as a "promised land" in which a new kingdom of God on earth might be erected, by the late seventeenth century, such expectations had been eroded by an expanding and increasingly diverse population. For some—namely, those urbanized individuals and families involved in trade, shipbuilding, and pub keeping (to mention but a few)—the experience of colonial life had paid fat dividends. For others, especially the agrarian farming class, early expectations of a land of plenty and prosperity had given way to a grim reality of shrinking landholdings and decreased profits. Historical research on the Salem trials suggests that the accusers and accused tended to fall on either side of this socioeconomic line: accusers tended to be the children of downtrodden, embittered farming families, while those accused tended to be either the relatively affluent residents of port towns or traditional social outcasts (targeted for racial background or allegedly immoral conduct). Still others among the accused had been involved in interpersonal disputes with the families of the afflicted. Add to this deep anxieties about conflicts with Native Americans, fear of contagious disease, and unease about the future political independence of the colony, and the proverbial table is set for rampant scapegoating: in all cases, those accused at Salem may be thought of as convenient targets for malaise and anger that had few, if any, other outlets. Whatever their real historical foundations, the 1692 persecutions remain an enigma in the public imagination. Many continue to ask such questions as, who were the witches? Were they real? Were innocents targeted? Did the devil really live in Salem? Does the devil continue to plague our society today? For the anthropologist of modern popular culture, the persistent narrative of Satan worship—and the alleged witchcraft it provokes—as an explanation of misfortune is at least as interesting as are questions about the objective reality of witches. If we strongly suspect that witchcraft accusations are one outcome of complex and troubling social and cultural circumstances, as the Salem events suggest, then why do such explanations continue to have power over the public imagination? Although diverse in their origins and assumptions, the articles in Part Five have in common the idea that modern allegations or defense of witchcraft are being made by a wide variety of people addressing a range of social, economic, medical, and cultural circumstances. Reading between the lines, these articles illustrate how witchcraft fears tend to arise in social environments of severe stress in which there seem to be no immediate explanations or resolutions. In times of cultural uncertainty—such as those brought on by natural disasters, epidemics, warfare, or deep epistemological and political divisions—most, if not all, cultural systems of meaning provide ways of accounting for and symbolically resolving endemic and destructive problems (that is, by identifying and punishing those responsible). These articles, then, do more than merely describe unusual events or arcane religious practices; in giving voice to beliefs about the reality of witchcraft, these discussions tend to lend credence to witchcraft as both a form of explanation and a "real" cultural practice—even when their authors don't intend for them to do so. A faint, if inconsistent, pattern is thus discernable among these and the other reports included in this part.

On one hand, reports of Satanic witchcraft lend weight to widespread assumptions about the "rational" world in which allegedly modern, ethical, and (mainly) Christian Americans live. We, modern Americans, are thus better, on the one hand, than our ancestors who believed in the power of witchcraft 300 years ago. It is as if to say that these things happened in 1692 among us (at Salem) but they could never happen now—as a society, we are evolved, mature, and "disenchanted" (to use a term popular among historians). In the modern world, the implication is that such superstitions are relegated to various forms of popular entertainment—television, movies, fiction, electronic games, and so on.

On the other hand, such reports have a second, no less significant effect: they feed an enduring, if mostly unspoken, uncertainty about what really happened at Salem and what really happens in the world today. For many people, religion is serious business—the Bible and some clergy speak of demons and witchcraft, so on what grounds should these stories be dismissed? In recent years, self-declared witches and Satanists have emerged out of the shadows, discarding their original 1960s countercultural trappings for the sake of political and cultural activism. In the twenty-first century, witches of various new religious traditions—represented in this part by Wicca and Satanism—seek to take their place in the theoretically pluralistic tradition of American religion. While we need not accept their beliefs at face value, the rest of us should at least entertain the following claims: Is Satanic witchcraft a real phenomenon and, consequently, a logical explanation for unfortunate events, great and small?

As it happens, there is a solid basis for this discussion, although the particulars are probably not what most Americans imagine. In fact, many scholars of "new religious movements" (a.k.a. NRMs or alternative religions) devote much of their careers to the study of various strains of contemporary witchcraft. At the risk of overgeneralization, NRMs are religions that have come into existence in the context of (and often in response to) various problems associated with what historians call "late modernity"—an epoch that is a complex outcome of, among others, new forms of industry and flows of goods, services, and personnel; complex forms of social stratification; deepening and expansive urbanization; and the fragmentation of identities through digital and modern communication and entertainment. These problems may generally be glossed by the term "social anomie"—that is, a widespread rupture between the world as it is promised and expected, and the real world as it confronts people in the experience of life. Although the term "new religious movement" implies a clean break with some past religious form, this is seldom the case. Most American NRMs build on either conventional world religions, such as Christianity (taking the form of new denominations and sects), or on the traditional religions of immigrant communities (for instance, branches of Buddhism and Hinduism brought by immigrants from the mid-twentieth century). Other NRMs (for instance the Raëlians, the tragic Heaven's Gate, and—especially—the Church of Scientology) find new meaning in hybrids of science and science fiction, often imbued with innovations proclaimed by a charismatic founder-leader. Still others, such as those discussed in readings in this part—(Wicca and Satanism, especially)—derive ideas from global mythology and the occult to provide a basis for religious commitment and ritual; they also provide a model and justification for the practice of witchcraft. So, exactly who are these flesh-and-blood witches who dwell among us?

Although space precludes lengthy discussion of these groups, it's useful to point out a few general features. The term "neo-pagan" may be used to gloss an eclectic range of groups whose members share some (but not all) transcendent beliefs, activities, and values—in particular, a commitment to ecological awareness, pre- and non-Christian traditions, and (often) feminist principles. Additionally, neo-pagans tend toward a general worldview in which all parts of reality are entangled by way of transcendent power, which makes it possible for practitioners to work "magick" (a term coined by forerunner Aleister Crowley). The word "Wiccan," for example, is derived from an Old English word related to the verb "bend" and associated with objects that bend and twist, such as tree branches. It thus suggests the image of witches manipulating and twisting mysterious forces of the universe. Diverse neo-pagan cultures venerate a great variety of transcendent beings, many of which are drawn from Celtic, Scandinavian, Near Eastern, Hindu, and Native American mythology. Practitioners assume a ubiquitous power at work in the natural universe that can be manipulated by all people to achieve real-world objectives (note that this is the traditional definition of magic discussed earlier). For Wiccans and other neo-pagans, such objectives are typically of a personal nature and patently benign: in common with people everywhere, they seek things like health, prosperity in jobs and romance, and protection for their children. Individuals who become "witches" must be of a generally harmonious mindset and disposition, however, in relation both to the natural world around them and to the universal properties of male and female—symbolic of the powers of procreation and fertility.

Modern witchcraft's generally peaceful objectives and practices do not preclude objections from religious traditionalists, however, who fear "occult" forces and the waning influence of Christian tradition. Critics of Wicca have also been known to espouse a kind of cultural snobbery in which the "strange" ritual activities, unconventional dress, and mystical beliefs are something of an embarrassment. This type of reaction is illustrated in this part by Reading 5.2: Fairbanks's profile of Pauline Hoffman—a Wiccan witch pressured to resign from her position as a dean at St. Bonaventure University—a Catholic institution. The ambivalence displayed even by this academic institution toward Hoffman reveals something of the complexity of modern witchcraft and the broader response to it, in that anyone who openly espouses stigmatized and stereotyped religious commitments (as opposed to the cynicism implied by clichés and cartoonish ideas about witches—all perfectly above board) is deserving of contempt. Much smaller than Wicca, but apparently growing by the day, is one new branch of Satanism: the Satanic Temple. Despite the claims of various Christian churches, organized Satanism has only existed from the mid-1960s. Its first formal expression, the Church of Satan (founded in 1966 by the notorious Anton LaVey) was in the main secretive, despite the outspokenness and showman instincts of its founder. Like Wiccans, these Satanists, too, claimed to have access to the powers inherent in the natural universe. In contrast to Wiccans, for whom an ethic of "do no harm" is central to their creed, from LaVey onward, most Satanists have embraced a philosophy of what might be called enlightened selfishness. For many Satanists, the most important feature of the human experience is carnality—the animalistic impulse to indulge all wants and cravings without concern for traditional religious doctrine and moral teaching. These, Satanists believe, are truly immoral institutions that prevent human beings from living out their true potential as earthly creatures. The majority of religious people, so the argument goes, are foolish, delusional, or insufficiently strong to stand up to such powerful institutions. This is why Satanism, according to Satanists themselves, appeals to true individualists, those unafraid to pursue their human vocation. Times have changed, however, and as Reading 5.4 makes clear, at least some twenty-first-century Satanists are not afraid to be provocative. In enacting their "pink mass" over the grave of a notoriously conservative Christian's mother, members of the Salem–based Satanic Temple (founded in 2012) managed to both enrage residents of a small Mississippi town and make a nationally felt political statement about the separation of church and state and gay rights. Subsequent assertions that the provocateurs would be arrested rang hollow and were perhaps designed more for impression management than to describe real law enforcement activity. That the Satanic Temple's witchcraft ritual—apparently designed to magically turn the deceased "gay for all eternity"—was taken seriously by frightened townsfolk speaks volumes about continuing twenty-first-century perceptions that witchcraft is the devil's work. Similar fears were doubtless stoked (at least for some) by the same institution the following year when Temple members unveiled plans to erect a statue of Baphomet (a horned goat-man symbol embraced by many Satanists) on the grounds of the Oklahoma state legislature—right next to a monument to the Ten Commandments. This unlikely pairing—intended to reinforce a sense that US religion is not "established" and that what was permissible for one should be permissible for all—made the Satanic Temple an unlikely key player in the ongoing debate between partisans of "Christian America," on one hand, and defenders of separation of church and state on the other. What Temple members had not anticipated was an outpouring of public sympathy for their position—even from Christians concerned with the implications of any single religion's influence on the institutions of the state.

As the readings in this part suggest, the witches studied by NRM scholars are hardly the mysterious hags of Shakespearian drama, let alone the Satanic minions imagined by a credulous seventeenth-century American public. Rather, they are individuals who create new forms of religious expression modeled on a wide variety of beliefs about the transcendent world. Many seek to revive what they view as "traditional" visions of who witches are and what witchcraft power was all about *before* they were tarnished by Christian moralizing and absolutism. Modern witches, in this regard, exist in the hundreds of thousands and are scattered around the world (although the major groupings thus far studied are linked to European peoples and diasporas). In contrast to the dread nightmares of societies, past and present, for whom witches were an imagined threat to individuals and communities, most members of contemporary witchcraft communities assert their benign status and generally claim a right to practice their faith in the face of much social ostracism and misunderstanding. The articles in part five provide us with a glimpse into a world of unconventional religious practices that, when examined in detail, look fairly familiar in terms of what they offer observers of human spirituality more broadly. Although the readings that follow represent only a narrow sliver of print media reportage concerning perceptions of witchcraft in the modern world, they suffice to give readers a sense of the range of the contradictions and inconsistencies embedded in witchcraft as a form of cultural explanation. It is equally clear that in the twenty-first century, the idea of witchcraft remains popular and compelling for many around the world and that new media technologies do not so much discourage or dispel such beliefs as encourage, spread, and even normalize them. Even in the halls of the US Capitol, as late as 2014, the specter of witchcraft was floated by a conservative bishop as part of a prayer for the nation. America, Bishop Angel Nunez claimed, risked losing God's divine protection if such devilry wasn't eliminated. In considering carefully the various fears and perspectives enlivening such rhetoric, readers might use the unusual events described in these articles as a lens through which to better understand how we think about others who are somehow different from us—physically, culturally, and morally. Perhaps as students of magic, witchcraft, and religion, we, too, should learn the lessons of 1692 Salem.

The NRA's Warning About Witchcraft and Gun Control May Not Be as Bizarre as You Think

By David Z. Morris

T HE NATIONAL RIFLE ASSOCIATION ISSUED A seemingly bizarre warning about witchcraft and gun control on Twitter over the weekend.

In the tweet, the NRA asked: "Have you ever wondered what happens when witchcraft intersects with gun control? Witch spells are cast onto POTUS and the NRA." The organization further pledged: "When fighting for freedom, the NRA doesn't get involved in witchcraft. We prefer education, political activism, and grassroots."

The phrasing of the tweet, which seemed to imply a real fear of witchcraft, has triggered a wave of mockery online. One critic of the anti-gun control organization asked: "Did you guys get hacked or are you legit this crazy?" Another observed that "the gun fetishists have started ranting about witches. This should end well."

But the message was more grounded in reality than it might have seemed. It linked to a report from the NRA's Institute for Legislative Action about self-described witches conducting actual rituals in Washington, D.C. "Witch" is a term often used for adherents of present-day Paganism, a nature-worshiping practice which has been recognized by Federal agencies including the Department of Defense. According to the Pew Research Center on Religion and Public Life, Pagans make up 0.3% of the American population, or close to 1 million individuals.

The NRA's report was based on a story from the Pagan website Wildhunt. org. According to that story, a group of eight witches conducted a "binding ritual" against President Trump last Februrary and later performed a similar ritual against the NRA, which was filmed for a forthcoming short documentary. The ritual, according to Wild Hunt, included an invocation with the lines "We curse you, merchants of mayhem, profiteers of pain, dealers of death, you who fatten on the blood of innocents and feast like demons on their corpses … May every mother's cry be a bullet to your heart." It also reportedly featured ritual objects including a five-dollar bill painted with "NRA" in red, intended to symbolize blood.

The NRA's response says that a Pagan ritual is a fair symbol for gun-control advocacy, which "is based mainly on magical thinking." Critics, though, seem to have read the NRA's tweet in light of the organization's strong links to evangelical Christianity. Evangelicals themselves often express literal belief in witchcraft and magic, but regard them as the work of the Devil—as seen, for instance, in persistent evangelical calls to ban the Harry Potter book series. Some respondents to the original tweet seemed to be of this mindset.

In the end, the NRA may be less anxious about real-world Pagan rituals, than eager to stoke the anxieties of a subset of gun-control advocates. That highlights a reality that's scarier than any mystical invocation—the deep ideological and cultural divides in American life. The level of disagreement between conservatives and liberals on government's role, and even on basic values, has been intensifying for years. Surveys have shown that divide deepening particularly sharply under President Trump.

It's distressing but barely surprising, then, that two groups of Americans would regard one another's political and religious beliefs as outright evil.

"Angry … Confused and Hurt": Wiccan Professor Sues St. Bonaventure

By Phil Fairbanks

PAULINE HOFFMANN RESIGNED HER POST AS dean of St. Bonaventure University's communication school, but says she did it under pressure.

She also claims the school denied her a promotion to provost, the university's highest academic position.

Why?

Hoffmann says it is because she is a woman and Wiccan.

In a lawsuit filed in Buffalo federal court, the St. Bonaventure professor—she is still on the faculty there—claims her religion and gender played a role in her forced resignation as dean and her failure to win a promotion she feels she deserved.

She is seeking her job back, lost pay and an unspecified amount in damages.

"I was angry but also confused and hurt," Hoffmann said of her treatment by the school's leadership. "It was like someone telling you, 'Don't be you.'"

A St. Bonaventure spokesman declined to comment Thursday, noting that the issue is a personnel matter and now in litigation.

In court papers, Hoffmann said the university was aware of her religion, but things turned bad in the fall of 2011 when she made it clear she intended to speak about Wicca with the student television station.

"They always want to talk to the witches at Halloween," she said of the student media at St. Bonaventure, "and I just wanted to give the school a heads up."

Pauline Hoffmann says she was removed from a department chairmanship at St. Bonaventure because she's a woman and Wiccan. (John Hickey/Buffalo News)

A few months later, then-Provost Michael J. Fischer approached her and demanded she sign a document vowing to uphold Catholic values, she claims in the suit.

"I asked him, 'Would this be happening if I was Jewish?'" she said during an interview Thursday. "And he said probably not."

Hoffmann said Fischer also told her, "You might not want to be so overt about being a witch if you want to move up."

Hoffmann said she was the only faculty member asked to sign the school's "morals code" and that made her angry.

"I just wanted to explain what Wicca was," she said, "but no one seemed to want to hear about it."

The lawsuit claims Sister Margaret Carney, then president of the university, knew about Hoffmann's religion early on but came to regret making her dean.

"I took a big chance hiring you as a Wiccan," Carney told her, according to the suit.

Hoffmann said the consequences of her decision to speak publicly about her religion quickly became apparent—she was denied the provost job and eventually forced to resign as dean.

The suit suggests Carney was instrumental in Hoffmann's resignation and claims current Provost Joseph Zimmer was told to "solve the Pauline problem."

The suit also claims Michael Hoffman, vice provost and chief information officer, told her, "Sister Margaret really has it in for you."

Hoffmann's lawyers said their client's case is not an isolated one and noted that, in their office, which represents only employees, the number of religious discrimination cases has more than doubled in the past year.

"People have a fear about that which they don't understand," said Lindy Korn, one of Hoffmann's attorneys.

Richard Perry, another of her lawyers, said Hoffmann's case will try to answer the question they always ask in discrimination cases: Why?

"We need to know why the employer did what they did," Perry said. "What was the 'Pauline problem?'"

Perry and Korn said their client is seeking a remedy that could range from monetary damages or diversity training to a more creative "symbolic apology." Korn mentioned a donation to an organization advocating religious tolerance as one example.

There is no doubt in Hoffmann's mind that her religion and gender were a big part of the "Pauline problem" and that she never would have been forced to resign if she were anything but Wiccan.

Raised in a Christian household, she learned about Wicca as an undergraduate student at St. Bonaventure—founded to promote a Catholic-Franciscan education—and found it to be a comfortable fit for her.

"Ironically, St. Bonaventure made me a witch," she said with a laugh.

When asked what she would have told university leaders if they had listened to her take on Wicca, she said she would have told them it's "a very natural religion."

"Our credo is, 'Do what you will but harm none,'" she said.

Thomas Missel, St. Bonaventure's chief communications officer, would not comment on the allegations Thursday.

"Since this is both a personnel and legal matter," Missel said in a statement, "it's not our policy or appropriate for the university to comment on the case."

Hoffmann, meanwhile, intends to carry on with her work as a professor in the Jandoli School of Communication.

"I do actually love my job," she said. "I love the students and I love interacting with my colleagues. And that's not going to change because of this."

There Weren't Any Witches in Salem in 1693. But There Sure Are Now.

By Tara Isabella Burton

S ALEM, MASSACHUSETTS—IT IS NIGHTFALL IN Salem, the week before Halloween. A woman who looks to be in her 70s sits in the bar of the Hawthorne Hotel sporting a novelty witch hat. Her male companion wears a spiderweb tie. Along the lawn at Washington Square, another tourist tugs at her companion's sleeve as she considers another destination for their week. "But it's not *spooky* like this place, right?" she asks.

At Pastime 32, a vintage-inspired craft shop just off Essex Street, a shopkeeper in velvet gives visitors advice about practicing magic. "Witchcraft is more of a life-style now than a religion," she says. She recommends that they read a BuzzFeed article to that effect. "So if a spell works it works." In the old days, she tells them, you might have had to resort to the formal magic kept in some arcane spell book. But now, she adds brightly, you can just check out Witch Instagram for ideas.

Along the narrow, red brick street in the pedestrianized heart of town, T-shirt stalls alternate with New Age storefronts selling herbs, tinctures, and Tarot cards.

Two girls fixate on the shirts. "Look! I got *stoned in Salem*." One pauses for a second. "Get it? Stoned?" She rolls her eyes, and explains to her friend what it means to stone somebody in order to execute them.

These tourists are just some of the million-odd who come to Salem each year. Destination Salem's Stacia Cooper says these tourists come to visit sites and museums associated with the Salem Witch Trials, where 20 people, mostly women, were executed on suspicion of witchcraft after an outbreak of mass hysteria in 1692 through 1693. Some visitors come for the "spooky" atmosphere. Others come, often with school groups, to learn more about a particularly brutal time in American history. And others still come because they identify as witches or practitioners of magic to pay tribute to a place that, for some, has become a source of spiritual pilgrimage.

The difference in their approach, and the myriad differing narratives around the trials available across town, reveal how powerful—and how diffuse—the story of the Salem Witch Trials really is. Is it a story about the dangers of superstition? About what happens when people let fear take over their lives? About misogyny and men policing women's identities? The different ways in which Salem's residents tell and retell the Salem narrative can tell us as much about 20th and 21st century America as they can about New England in 1693.

T-shirts with novelty slogans relating to witchcraft are common in Salem. Tara Isabella Burton

A Range of Political and Social Groups Have Interpreted Salem Differently

For Salem's 40,000 residents, particularly those who make their living through witch-related tourism, it can be a challenge to balance the historic narrative of the Salem Witch Trials with the powerful mythology that has surrounded it.

Between 1692 and 1693, 19 people were hanged, and one crushed to death, ostensibly for the civil crime of practicing malevolent witchcraft, after an outbreak of mass hysteria. Chances are, none of those 20 people were witches—they all maintained their innocence, with the exception of Tituba, a local enslaved woman, whose confession may have been tortured out of her.

The majority of the Salem Witch Trials didn't even happen in Salem Town—what is known as Salem today—but in Salem Village, an inland hamlet that was renamed Danvers in 1752. And on top of all this, none of the accused witches were stoned or burned at the stake in Salem, either.

According to Smithsonian's Danny Lewis, the witch trials were, historically, a taboo subject within Salem; a reminder of a horrific aberration. But in the 20th century, interest in the Salem Witch trials as a pop culture phenomenon was renewed. Much of this began with Arthur Miller's 1953 play *The Crucible*. A retelling of the trials, the play was a coded indictment of the anti-communist hysteria of the 1940s and 1950s. Miller heavily implied that the accusers and magistrates of Salem were motivated by a combination of fear and greed, including a desire to seize the lands of the accused. The story of Salem, for Miller, was the story of any mass panic—how self-interested human use fear and panic to stoke "witch hunts" for personal gain.

Salem is full of witch and New Age shops. Tara Isabella Burton

Then came *Bewitched*. When the popular, proto-feminist supernatural sitcom filmed a portion of its seventh season here in 1970, the protagonist, Samantha, seemed to uphold this dominant narrative. Samantha, a "real" witch who has magically time-traveled back to 17th-century Salem, uses her powers to prove that the other accused witches were innocent, condemning the prejudices of those who thought otherwise.

But Bewitched also heralded a change in how people saw Salem. It became "Witch City." Witches were now in fashion, after all—in part because of Bewitched—and Salem's witch history could be monetized. And Salem could use the money. After centuries as a prosperous shipping port, Salem's fortunes were in decline. The "Witch Tourism" boom revitalized Salem. (In 2005, in commemoration of that boom, Salem erected a controversial statue of Samantha in the town's main square, raising more debates about the degree to which "pro-witch" aesthetics had coopted Salem's legacy).

By the '70s, after all, feminist and New Age movements alike had reappropriated elements of the Salem narrative as part of a wider interest in women's spirituality. For many, the so-called witches of Salem were victims of a male conspiracy. The Salem story was the story of earth-centered, "natural" female spirituality dominated by a group of misogynist men who sought to control them. Witchcraft was something to celebrate.

In 1970, witch Laurie Cabot opened Salem's first New Age shop and several others followed suit. The accused of 1692 may not have been witches, but they were nevertheless celebrated as martyrs: foremothers of a modern movement they themselves would almost certainly have disavowed.

Those two strands of historical narrative—Salem as a site of mass panic, and Salem as witch city—are factually opposed to each other. Kristina Stevick, artistic director of the Cry Innocent project, which lets people experience a mock witch trial, thinks it's utterly illogical. "A person can't both be innocent and a martyr. That narrative really puzzles me."

And both narratives are also at odds with the generic "spookiness" that makes up much of the town's touristic appeal, particularly in Halloween season. (Of Salem's 40,000 residents, between 800 and 1,600 identify as witches, with many working in or through the town's witch shops, or in witch-related tourism industries, such as the city's myriad magic-themed walking tours.

The economics of Salem witchery is often a sore subject for many. Sources speaking on background spoke of "witch wars" between rival shop proprietors as well as price-fixing of services like Tarot readings, while some sources I contacted for this article would only agree to be interviewed on the condition certain proprietors be excluded from my reporting. (I have not quoted any of them.)

In Salem, Accused "Witches" Are Both Innocents and Martyrs

Yet many of Salem's tourist attractions try to have it both ways.

Nowhere is that difficult balance more evident than at the Salem Witch Museum, which opened in 1972—soon after *Bewitched* put the show on the map. Located in a converted church off Salem Common, the Museum tells the story of the trials through a combination of life-size wax statues, eerie sound effects, and a narrator who seems to have taken his delivery from Vincent Price.

He speculates about the devil "howling in the wind" (there's a menacing-looking statue of Satan himself), reports Puritan superstitions about witches' bacchanals, and captures each gory execution of the accused with thoroughly macabre sound effects. He walks us through a grisly narrative that combines kitschy "spookiness" with a some-what reductionist view of the trials, portraying them purely as the result of ignorant superstition, even as he uses the tropes of magic for dramatic effect. While the narrator reminds us that the mass panic was anything but supernatural, he leaves us with a distinctly Gothic ending, asking us to reflect on who the "real demons are" and "on whose side they are still working today."

The museum's second exhibit likewise tells us as much about 1970s New Age feminism as it does about the Salem Witch trials. Dedicated to the history of the witch from the pre-Christian era to the modern day, the museum (and its docents) tell a very clear-cut, if simplistic, narrative. Women, particularly midwives, were once "in touch with" the earth. They worshipped a pre-Christian Goddess. Once Christianity came to power, evil Christian men—"the Church"—were afraid of female power and tried to stamp it out. More wax figures present different visions of the witch: the angelic, beaming midwife, the green-faced crone we recognize from *The Wizard of Oz's* Wicked Witch of the West.

A timeline on one wall elides world history: We move swiftly from "Jesus Christ is crucified" to witch panics in 16th-century Scotland, with an implicit link between the two. A final tableau of two modern Wiccans invites us to learn more about this "ancient religion" and speak to its peace-loving practitioners. While the odd mention is made of the fact that Salem's witches were innocent, a less-careful viewer could easily come away with the idea that the accused of Salem *did* practice wholesome, nature-based magical traditions and worship a Goddess in secret, and that this is, in fact, a good thing.

Historicity, in this exhibition, seems less important than symbolism, celebrating the witch as a symbol of maligned womanhood. Wicca, far from being an "ancient religion," only dates back to the 1950s, which the museum never mentions. And although the "green-skinned witch" as a trope only dates back to 1939's *Wizard of Oz*, when dyeing Margaret Hamilton's skin was a novel special effect to capitalize on the then-new use of Technicolor, my docent presents several other options as equally valid. Were witches green-skinned because of their use of herbs, she asks aloud? A witch who visited the exhibition, she tells us, sees the green as important symbolism: It is the bruises left upon her by intolerant Christian men who beat her for her independent thought.

It's a powerful exhibit, to be sure, but one with an agenda. And it raises questions about more than just what happened in 1692. Rather, it challenges us to think about whether history can or should be rewritten, or reimagined, if the myths it presents to us can inspire positive change. Does a woman's personal reaction to a figure of a witch—her intuitive feeling that her face is the color of bruises—belong in a museum alongside, say, actual documents of the trials themselves?

For Others, Salem Is about Learning to Think Historically— and Critically—about Challenging Narratives

Stevick, at least, has her doubts. Her Cry Innocent project is an immersive theatre experience that challenges audience members to participate in a mock witch trial. It is designed to help audiences understand the mentality of the witch trials, ideally without projecting a contemporary narrative upon it. The project plays an exceedingly necessary role in Salem, since, Stevick says, the trials have become a lightning rod for different, often ahistorical, interpretations of what happened in 1693.

She counts off the most popular misconceptions: "That it's all about land-grabbing, that it's just about misdirected misogyny [against accused women], that Puritans were just stupid and superstitious, that those who died were the spiritual foremothers of the Wicca movement ..."

Stevick says she sympathizes with such interpretations up to a point. But, ultimately, each narrative fails to appreciate the "cocktail of factors" that made Salem a lightning rod for hysteria in the late 17th century. The dangers of foreign invasion, tensions within the community over religious observance, the adversarial relationship between the insular Salem Village and the wealthier Salem Town, tensions over the use of folk magic, and various waves of outbreak of illness all contributed to an incident that was about so much more than mere superstition or mere misogyny or mere anything.

Often, Stevick says, people are reluctant to abandon their preconceived narratives about the trials. She recalls an incident that happened the previous week with a middle school group that had booked a Cry Innocent show.

"They had a reductionist idea of what the witch hunt hysteria was about and thought that this was their opportunity to bring down the magistrate," Stevick said. Rather than looking through the historical evidence presented during the show, she said, the students derailed the show with

Margaret McGilvray in rehearsal, performing from her latest Tarot-inspired piece of performance art at The Witcher.
Tara Isabella Burton

unrelated questions and preconceived judgments, making the show "a little bit distressing" for the actors.

She recalls the students' teacher was taken aback by the complexity with which the Cry Innocent cast wanted to approach the 17th-century Puritan mindset. "She wanted this to be an opportunity for the students to take down the patriarchy, which I could relate to, but it's not what's happening here."

It's a shame, says Stevick, because ultimately developing a more complex understanding of history is necessary if one is to avoid repeating it. "What I would hope is that a person who has had 45 minutes to flirt with a 17th-century English mindset … would understand why a person *might* accuse somebody of witchcraft."

It is that, she says, rather than a preconceived narrative, that has the most power to inspire change.

Only once audience members learn to empathize with people from the past whose attitudes and preconceptions might be different from their own, she says, audience members can ask themselves: "How can I use this newfound imagination … to try and look into my current political situation? … Our country is in a fragile dangerous place [right now] and we need to be extremely careful that a great tragedy doesn't happen." She corrects herself. "*Another* great tragedy."

For Contemporary Witches, Salem's Magic Is Still "Mysterious"

Among Salem's practicing witches, the place's magic transcends its history. Margaret McGilvray, who runs The Witchery, equal parts magic shop and experimental performance art space, says that—despite the innocence of Salem's original "witches"—she's always felt a preternatural connection to the place. Visiting the Salem Witch Museum as a child, McGilvray says, she found herself identifying with the accused.

"I came home to my mom and said 'Ma, I think I'm a witch.'" She recognizes that the witches of Salem denied being witches up through their last breaths, but nevertheless finds in Salem a kind of spiritual home; a place where she can connect with and collaborate with like-minded practitioners. Part of it, she acknowledges, is "commercialism"—if you're a witch, Salem is a great place to make a living—but part of it is more profound.

"There is something just mysterious about Salem as a gut level," McGilvray says.

And Salem's draw, for other witches, has transcended its witchy history, becoming as much about the present as the past.

As the "witch aesthetic" becomes more popular as a cultural signifier—blending '70s-era New Age spirituality with left-wing activism and, at times, performative rebellion—Salem has become something of a hipster haven. In 2015, Salem's more eclectic, cluttered-looking witch shops were joined by the sleek, minimalist HausWitch (which itself started as an Instagram), where activist hours are on the schedule alongside Tarot salons and meditation classes. (Destination Salem's Cooper describes them as the "millennial" witch store).

These witches are attracted to what HausWitch worker Cheryl Rafuse calls the "good vibes" of Salem—a town whose witch traditions have given rise, in turn, to a thriving counterculture, and the creative community that comes with it—as to its history. So often Rafuse says, people visit out of interest in the "Witch City" only to fall in love with the place and joke about moving. "And then they end up moving here a year later."

Sure, she admits, she gets frustrated by the gimmicky aesthetic of some of the town's tourist traps. She points to the *Stoned in Salem* T-shirts as a particularly egregious example.

"There's a scene [in Salem] that's a little uncomfortable considering" the grotesque nature of the trials, Rafuse says.

"A *lot* uncomfortable," Erica Feldmann, the shop's owner, cuts in.

Rafuse continues, "the people we draw tend to be pretty woke, good-vibe-y people, or at least looking for something here [that's] at least not gimmicky. We have that 'Witch City' vibe that people love … but [when] people try to make light of history"—mocking or joking about those that died—Rafuse and other shop workers actively work to discourage them.

Feldmann adds, "The world needed a place to celebrate the witch, and that ended up being Salem, and that has nothing to do with the witch trials."

Ultimately, Salem's History Might Be Less Important Than Its Symbolism

The "true history" of Salem, in other words, might be almost irrelevant. A combination of economics and mythology have made Salem a location of pilgrimage for those who identify with the accused of 1693, whether they are witches themselves, feminists drawn to the narrative of wrongly accused women, or just ordinary people drawn to the story of those penalized for being a little bit different. Even Stevick acknowledges that even the more ahistorical elements of Salem's mythology—that it was all about misogyny, say—might be powerful narratives of support for people who need them most.

She recalls an episode years ago, when she was portraying the character of Bridget Bishop—the woman on trial for witchcraft. A student group had come in, and a shy girl in the audience got up to ask a question in defense of Bishop. Stevick can't remember precisely what the question was, but "I could tell that she was really nervous to speak in public, she was shaking … I remember it being an intense moment—the air was thick."

A few years later, when the teacher brought in another group, she and Stevick discussed that day. The teacher told Stevick the girl was famously shy, without many friends.

"It turned out that she was pregnant," Stevick remembers. "[She was] facing this extra level of slut-shaming and all this stuff at school … [the Cry Innocent experience] had given her the extrovertive *oomph* to get up and say something. And that moment had been a catharsis for her. And that touched me so deeply and made me think: That's why I love doing this type of theater. That kind of catharsis is okay. Even while it might not be quite the right narrative, I'm okay with people saying, 'Yeah Bridget! Go Bridget!' too."

There is, in all this, a degree of irony. A town once derided for the damaging aftereffects of religion and superstition has now remade itself in the image of its own new myths.

At Salem's Witch Museum, the narrator tells us—with more than a little derision—that the Puritans were a superstitious people. They made up stories to explain the world around them, narratives that would make the chaos of their existence make sense. But if Salem can teach us anything, not a lot has changed.

Austin Chapter of the Satanic Temple Gains Followers, Gives Back

By Rolando Hernandez

IN APRIL 2019, THE IRS RECOGNIZED the Satanic Temple as an official house of worship that now has the tax benefits and protection from discrimination that other religions have had. The Satanic Temple is the first Satanic religion to gain this exemption from the IRS.

Amber Rex, a national council member of the Satanic Temple said they weren't able to receive the same benefits, such as grants, that other religious offices get because they don't have a tax-exempt code.

"We weren't able to do a lot of things," Rex said. "We just want a seat at the table."

Marshall Smith, business administrator with the First Baptist Church of Austin, said these nonprofit tax codes help provide the church with additional funding to give back to the community.

"We help provide common things the city or county doesn't provide," Smith said.

At first, Rex said temple members believed the temple should pay taxes but later realized it is only fair that the Satanic Temple be exempt, too, if other religious organizations aren't required to pay taxes.

With tax exemptions, Smith said the First Baptist Church of Austin was able to aid in the needs of the "underserved and homeless neighbors" by helping with things such as getting state-issued IDs and birth certificates so that they can apply for assistance and employment programs.

Photo Credit: Raquel Higine
Daily Texan Staff

However, the first Baptist Church isn't the only organization that helps the homeless. The Satanic Temple's Austin chapter has its own way of lending a hand.

Even before it was tax exempt, the Satanic Temple had been an active group in the community because of its beliefs. The Temple follows a set of seven fundamental tenets that encourage activism and community service, similar to other religious organizations.

Shelby Scates, the Austin chapter's co-head, said they host an annual Menstruatin' with Satan fundraiser to purchase feminine care products for women experiencing homelessness.

"This initiative was started to help disenfranchised groups that traditional churches don't normally help," Scates said.

Another ongoing project the Temple practices is collecting hygiene products for Stop Abuse For Everyone, a nonprofit that aids victims of sexual assault, domestic violence and children facing abuse. Scates said they have collection barrels throughout Austin at local businesses such as The Glass Coffin, a vampire-themed antique and oddities shop.

Scates also said the Temple also holds an annual unbaptism where people who feel they were baptized without consent can revoke that.

"You either pay the door fee or donate a case of water," Scates said. "We're raising bottles of water, it's a baptism—kinda symbolic."

Natalie Freeburg, the community relations and volunteer coordinator at Front Steps, said the Temple raised around 500 gallons of water last year for the organization, the nonprofit that manages the Austin Resource Center for the homeless. Freeburg also said the Satanic Temple gifted more than 4,000 water bottles to its clients experiencing homelessness.

"They are proactive, kind and committed to helping others," Freeburg said.

With the IRS exemption, Scates said the Austin chapter can hopefully do more.

"Having this official recognition is vital for the autonomy of our religion as a whole," Scates said.

The Rise of Progressive Occultism

By Tara Isabella Burton

B ACK IN MARCH 2019, AN ELECTED government representative shared something personal about her spiritual identity. Not a preferred Bible verse or
a conversion story. Rather, progressive New York Representative Alexandria
Ocasio-Cortez shared her birth-time with a self-described psychic and astrol-
oger, Arthur Lipp-Bonewits, who in turn shared her entire birth chart with
what can only be described as Astrology Twitter.

Astrology Twitter went wild. So did the mainstream media, with outlets
from Vox to The Cut to Allure speculating about what Ocasio-Cortez's astro-
logical chart could tell us about her fitness for political office. "AOC's Aries
Moon indicates that she's emotionally fed by a certain amount of independence,
self-determination, and spontaneity," concluded Allure's Jeanna Kadlec. "But that
independence always finds a way home." Meanwhile, Lipp-Bonewits told The
Cut's Madeleine Aggeler that the stars predicted that Ocasio-Cortez's "career
in politics is likely to last the rest of her life."

Ocasio-Cortez's decision to share her birth-time with Lipp-Bonewits might
be an unprecedented move for a political figure—Hillary Clinton famously
avoided the question, sparking years of debate among astrologers. But it was also
a canny one. Twenty-nine percent of Americans say they believe in astrology,
according to a 2018 Pew poll, while just 22 percent of Americans call themselves mainline Protestants.

More importantly, however, AOC's gambit taps into the way in which progressive millennials have appropriated the rhetoric, imagery, and rituals of what
was once called the "New Age"—from astrology to witchcraft—as both a political and spiritual statement of identity.

For an increasing number of left-leaning millennials—more and more of
whom do not belong to any organized religion—occult spirituality isn't just
a form of personal practice, self-care with more sage. Rather, it's a metaphysical canvas for the American culture wars in the post-Trump era: pitting the

self-identified Davids of seemingly secular progressivism against the Goliath of nationalist evangelical Christianity.

There's the coven of Brooklyn witches who publicly hexed then-Supreme Court candidate Brett Kavanaugh to the acclamation of the thousands-strong "Magic Resistance"—anti-Trump witches (among them: pop singer Lana del Rey) who used at-home folk magic to "bind" the president in the months following his inauguration. There are organizations like The Satanic Temple —newly featured in Penny Lane's 2019 documentary Hail Satan—a "nontheistic religion" and activist group that uses its religious status to demand for its black-robe-clad members the same protections afforded to Christians in the hopes of highlighting the ridiculousness of faith-based exceptions (Satanic prayer in schools, say). There are dozens of Trump-era how-to spellbooks that blend folk magic with activist practice: the 2018 anthology The New Arcadia: A Witch's Handbook to Magical Resistance; Michael Hughes's 2018 Magic for the Resistance: Rituals and Spells for Change; David Salisbury's 2019 Witchcraft Activism: A Toolkit for Magical Resistance (Includes Spells for Social Justice, Civil Rights, the Environment, and More); and Sarah Lyons's forthcoming Revolutionary Witchcraft: A Guide to Magical Activism. There are hundreds of thousands of users of witch-popular blogging platforms like Tumblr and Instagram, which at the moment boasts 8.5 million photographs hashtagged "#witch."

And there are the ubiquitous feel-good articles in progressive-friendly millennial outlets, such as Marie Claire's "This Is How Real-Life Resistance Witches Say They're Taking Down the Patriarchy" and Broadly's "How the Socialist Feminists of WITCH Use Magic to Fight Capitalism," packaging the connection between left-wing politics and occultism as an integral part of the progressive millennial experience. (There has also been an inevitable trickle effect: In late 2018, high street makeup chain Sephora announced that it would be selling a $42 "Starter Witch Kit," complete with burnable white sage and tarot cards; they later recanted after witches accused them of culturally appropriating witch practice for profit).

As an aesthetic, as a spiritual practice, and as a communal ideology, contemporary millennial "witch culture" defines itself as the cosmic counterbalance to Trumpian evangelicalism. It's at once progressive and transgressive, using the language of the chaotic, the spiritually dangerous, and (at times) the diabolical to chip at the edifices of what it sees as a white, patriarchal Christianity that has become a de facto state religion.

They have a point. White evangelicals, after all, ushered Donald Trump into the White House. Since 2016, they have been the only religious bloc to consistently support Trump, and Trump has responded in kind, repaying his evangelical base with all-but-unprecedented access to the corridors of power and—no less importantly—with his Administration's rhetoric. Bastions of Moral Majority-era evangelical institutions—Jerry Falwell's Liberty University, for instance—have dedicated time and money to promoting projects like the Liberty-funded film The Trump Prophecy, which heavily implies that

Trump is a modern-day King Cyrus, specifically chosen by God to fulfill His vision for Israel. Members of Trump's unofficial evangelical advisory council, such as Robert Jeffress and Paula White, have publicly stated that God chose Trump to be President—and that we owe him obeisance as a result of divine decree. Even more secular members of the Trump Administration have leaned heavily on the rhetoric of Christian nationalism. Both former Attorney General Jeff Sessions and former White House Press Secretary Sarah Huckabee Sanders invoked Romans 7:1-13—a plea for respecting earthly authority—to defend the Administration's family separation policy during the 2018 migrant crisis. The White House has consistently used religious rhetoric, in other words, to underpin its temporal aims.

Now, its opponents are doing the same.

Progressive occultism—the language of witches and demons, of spells and sage, of cleansing and bad energy, of star and signs—has become the de facto religion of millennial progressives: the metaphysical symbol set threaded through the worldly ethos of modern social justice activism. Its rise parallels the rise of the religious "nones," and with them a model of spiritual and religious practice that's at once intuitional and atomized. Twenty-three percent of Americans call themselves religiously unaffiliated, a number that spikes to 36 percent among millennials (Trump's white evangelical base, by contrast, only comprises about 17 percent of Americans). But tellingly, few among this demographic identify as atheists or agnostics. A full 72 percent of "nones" say they believe in God, or at least some kind of nebulously defined Higher Power; 17 percent say they believe in the Judeo-Christian God of the Bible. Suspicious of institutions, authorities, and creeds, this demographic is less likely to attend a house of worship, but more likely to practice the phenomenon Harvard Divinity School researchers Casper ter Kuile and Angie Thurston have termed "unbundling": a willingness to effectively "mix and match" spiritual, ritualistic, and religious practices from a range of traditions, divorced from their original institutional context. A member of this "remixed" generation, for example, might attend yoga classes, practice Buddhist meditation, read Tarot cards, cleanse their apartment with sage, and also attend Christmas carol concerts or Shabbat dinners. They might tap into the perceived psychic energy of their surroundings at a boutique fitness studio like SoulCycle, which openly bills itself as a "cult," and whose charismatic trainers frequently post spiritually tinged motivational mantras like "You were created by a purpose, for a purpose" on SoulCycle's social media platforms. The underpinnings of religious life—meaning, purpose, community, and ritual—are more likely than ever to come from diffuse traditions, or indeed no tradition at all.

Within this paradigm, the popularity of what might be termed "New Age" practices makes perfect sense. This umbrella movement, born in the counterculture of the 1960s, combined a variety of anti-authoritarian spiritual practices that stressed the primacy of the self, the power of intuition, the untrustworthiness of orthodox institutions, and the spiritual potential of the "forgotten"—often women. Reconstructionist pagan religions like Wicca—founded in the 1950s by Gerald Gardner, who dubiously claimed it was based on ancient Celtic traditions—grew popular with a demographic that felt marginalized by "traditional" organized religions. Central to most of these movements was the idea that the intuitional, usually female self could access a deeper truth than patriarchal religions like Christianity grasped. Power came from within, not outside. As one influential New Age practitioner put it in her 1982 book Dreaming the Dark: Magic, Sex, and Politics:

There are many names for power-from-within.... none of them entirely satisfying.... It could be called God—but the God of patriarchal religions has been the ultimate source and repository of power-over. I have called it immanence, a term that is truthful but somewhat cold and intellectual. And I have called it Goddess, because the ancient images, symbols and myths of the Goddess as birth-giver, weaver, earth and growing plant, wind and ocean, flame, web, moon and milk, all speak to me of the powers of connectedness, sustenance, and healing.

Still, throughout most of the New Age movement, the number of actual practitioners of Wicca were limited. In 1990, there were only about 8,000 self-identified Wiccans in America. But in the past few decades, those numbers have been growing: By 2001, there were 134,000, and by 2014, Pew data suggested that the combined number of pagans and Wiccans in America was over a million. Wicca, by that estimation, is technically the fastest-growing religion in America.

But contemporary witchcraft—the kind of occultism we see in Ocasio-Cortez's star chart and the hexing of Brett Kavanaugh—isn't limited to those who practice paganism or Wicca as a religion, with a well-structured set of metaphysical and magical assumptions. It appears far more often as a component of "unbundled" religious identity, where it is nearly always wedded to social justice activism. Like their New Age forebears, contemporary witches understand witchcraft as a practice for those on the societal margins, a reclamation of power for those disenfranchised by unjust or oppressive systems. While traditional New Age culture focused primarily on the experience of (usually white) women, contemporary witch culture frames itself as proudly, committedly intersectional: an umbrella community for all those pushed to the side by the dominant (white, straight, male, Christian) culture. Symbols and images of the uncanny, the demonic, and even the diabolical are recast as icons of the falsely accused, the wrongly blamed, the scapegoated.

"Who, exactly, is the witch," asks Kristin J. Sollee of the 2017 book Witches, Sluts, Feminists: Conjuring the Sex Positive—one of the many feminist witch texts to arise out of the Trump era. "She's Hecate, the ancient Greek goddess of the crossroads. She's Lilith, the blood-drinking demoness of Jewish mythology who refused to submit sexually to her husband.... She's Joan of Arc, the French military hero in white armor burned by her brethren for cross dressing and heresy.... She's Malala Yousafzai, the Pakistani teen shot for her feminist advocacy and awarded the Nobel Peace Prize.... she's every woman.... at once female divinity, female ferocity, and female transgression." Witchcraft is, in Sollee's reading, divorced from religious belief—Joan, a committed Christian, and Malala, an observant Muslim, might well have been horrified to find themselves lumped in with mythology's more nefarious blood-drinkers—and associated rather with a common, countercultural identity. Likewise, David Salisbury—author of the 2019 handbook Witchcraft Activism, which encourages readers to petition the Greek god Hermes to ensure that letters to congressional representatives have an effect—similarly casts witchcraft as the natural spiritual inheritance of cultural outsiders. "Witchcraft is the unconquerable shout at midnight," Salisbury writes. "It screams to be heard because it is the lighthouse for the voiceless."

Material witch culture—from books to magical paraphernalia—has likewise changed with the times. Any self-respecting witch looking to combine personal spirituality with intersectionality can, for example, pick up a Tarot deck like the one designed by queer illustrator Christy P. Road, which primarily depicts characters of color, sex workers, and non-binary characters, and is about "smashing systematic oppression, owning their truths, being accountable to the people and places that support them, and taking back a connection to their body that may have been lost through trauma or societal brainwashing." (There are so many queer-friendly Tarot decks out there that lesbian website Autostraddle made a full listicle of them in 2015.)

While New Age practitioners of the 1960s onward often characterized their practice as unfailingly benign—the karmic "Rule of Three," which predicted that any negative energy sent into the universe would reverberate threefold on a practitioner, was ubiquitous in neo-pagan circles—contemporary witch feminism rebrands occult darkness as a legitimate, even necessary response to a structural oppression. In one Brooklyn zine, author and non-binary witch Dakota Bracciale—co-owner of Catland Books, the occult store behind the Kavanaugh hexing—celebrates the potential of traditional "dark magic" and outright devil-worship as a levying force for social justice.

"There have been too many self-elected spokespersons for all of witchcraft," Bracciale writes, "seeking to pander to the masses and desperately conform to larger mainstream religious tenets in order to curry legitimacy. Witchcraft has largely, if not exclusively, been a tool of resilience and resistance to oppressive power structures, not a plaything for bored, affluent fools. So if one must ride into battle under the banner of the Devil himself to do so then I say so be it. The reality is that you can be a witch and worship the devil and have sex with demons and cavort through the night stealing children and burning churches. One should really have goals." As with the denizens of The Satanic Temple, Bracciale uses the imagery of Satanism as a direct attack on what he perceives as Christian hegemony. So too Jex Blackmore, a self-proclaimed Satanic feminist (and former national spokesperson for the Satanic Temple) who appeared in the Hail Satan? documentary performing a Satanic ritual involving half-naked worshippers and pigs' heads on spikes, announcing:

"We are going to disrupt, distort, destroy.... We are going to storm press conferences, kidnap an executive, release snakes in the governor's mansion, execute the president."

Bracciale and Blackmore's language might be extreme, but their overall ethos—that progressive activism demands a robust, cosmic-level, anti-Christian (or at least, anti-conservative, evangelical Christian) metaphysical and rhetorical grounding—has permeated activist culture more broadly. Last month, for example, when pro-choice advocates marched on the South Carolina State House to protest the Alabama abortion ban, protesters held signs identifying themselves as "the grandchildren of the witches you could not burn." (This phrase has also been spotted on placards at the annual Women's March). Millennial-focused sites like Vice's Broadly and Bust have sympathetically profiled the progressive potential of Satanic feminism in particular: One Broadly profile of an LA-based Satanic doo-wop band proclaims them "Feminist as fuck", while another piece attempts to rehabilitate the mythological demon Lilith as "a Chill Demon" and a "powerful figure with a continued relevance for women today."

Granted, most millennial denizens of "Witchblr" are more likely to cleanse their homes with sage, say, or practice mindfulness meditation than to cast a curse on Republican lawmakers. But the rhetorical and spiritual popularization of "resistance magic" in the age of Trump reveals the degree to which one of America's supposedly most "secular" demographics—urbane, progressive millennials—aren't quite so secular after all. From Tarot readings to spell craft, meditation to cursing, they're actively seeking out religious and spiritual traditions defined by their marginality—traditions that at once offer a sense of cosmic purpose and political justice against what they see as hegemonic power. These practices may be less established, and far more diffuse, than those offered by organized religion, but they offer adherents some of the same psychological effects: a committed and ideologically cohesive community, a sense of purpose both on a political battlefield and a mythic one.

The scholars Joshua Landry and Michael Saler call this quintessentially phenomenon "re-enchantment." In their 2009 book *The Re-Enchantment of the World: Secular Magic in a Rational Age,* they argue that we are seeing a resurgence in seemingly atheistic spaces of "a variety of secular and conscious strategies for re-enchantment, held together by their common aim of filling a God-shaped void." The contemporary millennial Left, increasingly alienated from a Christianity it sees as repressive, outmoded, and downright abusive, has used the language, the imagery, and the rituals of modern occultism to re-enchant its seeming secularism.

Followers of Ocasio-Cortez's star chart, contemporary witch feminists, serious proponents of Satanic feminism, and dabblers in Sephora-accessible Tarot cards alike all share both a hunger for the grounding effects of spiritual presence and a fervent conviction that personal spirituality should resist, rather than renew, the newly waning power of institutional religion. In this, they're finally following the playbook of their greatest foes. For decades, the Christian Right has been able to consistently mobilize its voters more successfully than most other religious groups, precisely because it raised the political stakes to a battle between Good and Evil, while the "religiously unaffiliated" have consistently failed to show up at the polls. In 2014, for example, "nones" made up 22 percent of the population, but just 12 percent of the voters; meanwhile, white evangelicals have consistently made up a quarter of voters, despite comprising 17 percent of the population. The proliferation of progressivism as a spiritual as well as political identity may well be the unifying force the Left needs to emerge as a bona fide demographic bloc.

Granted, these spiritual practices remain niche, even as their commercial manifestation becomes more commonplace. And their diversity and lack of shared metaphysical grounding —in part a function of millennial unbundledness—could constrain their ability to bring people together. Religious practices defined by intuition, rather than creed, may have a hard time calcifying members into an ideologically coherent group. But the fact that a religious impulse is fragmented and decentralized does not mean it is impotent: The Great Awakenings of the eighteenth and nineteenth centuries, not to mention the rise of the 1960s spiritual counterculture, began in just this way. And even mainstream progressives seem to be taking faith more seriously now than in the recent past—Pete Buttigieg, for instance, is quite open about his Christianity. It's impossible to know where these diffuse strains of pietism will ultimately lead. But at minimum, they suggest that secularization is not the inevitable or even the most logical endpoint for today's Left. Far from it. Rather, we're looking at a profoundly pagan form of re-enchantment.

Back in 1992, Christian broadcaster Pat Robertson warned of the dangers of feminism, predicting that it would induce "women to leave their husbands.... practice witchcraft, destroy capitalism and become lesbians." Many of today's witches would happily agree.

Discussion Questions

1. Why is modern paganism problematic for some nonpagans in US society?
2. What kinds of magical powers are manipulated by modern witches and for what purposes?
3. What role does the modern city of Salem play in the ideology of modern witchcraft? How does this contrast with the seventeenth-century vision of witches?
4. How do non- Satanic varieties of paganism compare with Satanism and Satanic activities?
5. What has the public and law enforcement response been to the recently raised profile of Satanism? Is this a positive development or not for US society?
6. How has the idea of witchcraft been invoked in relation to political and other public figures and organizations in the modern United States?
7. Considering the rise of the Satanic Temple, is it fair to say there is a place for Satanism in the tapestry of US religions? Why or why not?

Further Readings

Baker, Emerson W. *A Storm of Witchcraft: The Salem Trials and the American Experience.* Oxford: Oxford University Press, 2014.

This acclaimed book places the events of the 1692 witchcraft persecutions in the wider context of social, political, and religious developments in New England and Great Britain, and examines the legacy of the Salem trials in US public memory.

Berger, Helen A., ed. *Witchcraft and Magic: Contemporary North America.* Philadelphia: University of Pennsylvania Press, 2011.

This textbook introduces students to current forms of witchcraft activity in North America. Most especially, contributors offer analyses of such neo-pagan religions as Wicca, Satanism, African Caribbean traditions, neo-Nazi religion, and a variety of occult groups. Berger's volume is very useful for any student desiring a wide-ranging and jargon-free primer on the anthropology and social history of modern witchcraft religions.

Faxneld, Per, and Jesper Aa. Petersen, eds. *The Devil's Party: Satanism in Modernity.* Oxford: Oxford University Press, 2012.

A comprehensive and challenging collection of historical and sociological essays that delve into the murky, diverse, and often misunderstood world of Satanism and Satanists. Essays focus on such topics as the emergence of Satanic practice in the 1960s US counterculture, the progressive development of Satanic activities in the emerging world of online cultures, and the fringe connections between esoteric Satanism and extreme right-wing political groups.

Goodman, Felicitas D. *How About Demons? Possession and Exorcism in the Modern World.* Bloomington, IN: Indiana University Press, 1988.

This 1980s book on the folklore and anthropology of possession and exorcism remains one of the few cross-cultural studies available on the topic. Drawing on ethnographic examples from Japan, Brazil, Mexico, Africa, and popular US culture, Goodman (a professional folklorist and Ursuline nun) explores the phenomenon from the perspective of desiring to understand the role of trance and possession states in human culture.

Landry, Joshua, and Michael Saler. *The Re-Enchantment of the World: Secular Magic in a Rational Age*. Palo Alto: Stanford University Press, 2009.

This interdisciplinary work explores and critiques assumptions about the supposedly rational and scientized character of the modern world. In particular, Landry and Saler investigate the strategies various movements have used to replace discarded traditional faiths with new, enchanted forms of reasoning and practice.

Levack, Brian P., ed. *The Witchcraft Sourcebook*. 2nd ed. New York: Routledge, 2015.

This volume features a wide range of historically significant essays and documents (many of which are original sources) concerning mainly European and Euro-American varieties of belief in witches and witchcraft activities. These include trial records, theological and demonological sermons, and accounts of medieval and early modern witch hunts.

Lewis, James R., ed. *Magical Religion and Modern Witchcraft*. Albany, NY: SUNY Press, 1996.

Lewis's now-classic ethnological and historical portrait of contemporary witchcraft beliefs and practices covers a wide swath of the neo-pagan world from goddess and nature-focused spiritualities to Odinism and fascination with the occult. In contrast to similar scholarly volumes, he devotes extensive discussion to the connections and divergences between Christian and neo-pagan ethics and worldviews.

Rapley, Robert. *Witch Hunts: From Salem to Guantanamo Bay, Annotated Edition*. Montreal: McGill-Queen's University Press, 2007.

Rapley provides a comparative historical analysis of witch-hunting as a social practice, distinct from witches and witchcraft as real people and institutions. His study identifies patterns in social and cultural context across current and historical societies (ranging from the sixteenth through the twenty-first centuries) in which fear of witches emerges as a crucial social dynamic.

Sims, Jenn, ed. *The Sociology of Harry Potter: 22 Enchanting Essays on the Wizarding World*. Allentown, PA: Zossima Press, 2012.

A series of academic essays that place themes, events, and characters from J. K. Rowling's novels in the context of current issues and theoretical orientations (such as those concerning identity, technology, and social inequality) in the field of sociology.

Waldron, David. *The Sign of the Witch: Modernity and the Pagan Revival.* Durham, NC: Carolina Academic Press, 2008.

This study investigates the origins of contemporary ideas about the Western witch, illuminating the changing character of this symbol from early modern centuries through the contemporary era. Waldron's analysis culminates in an exploration of the neo-pagan and Wiccan religions of recent decades, which he shows to have transformed the earlier sinister symbolism of witchcraft into something more in keeping with postmodern culture.

Index

Printed in the USA
CPSIA information can be obtained
at www.ICGtesting.com
LVHW081942201123
764471LV00007B/40